DIGEST OF AMERICAN INDIAN LAW

DIGEST OF AMERICAN INDIAN LAW:
Cases and Chronology

H. Barry Holt
Gary Forrester

Fred B. Rothman & Co.
Littleton, CO 80127
1990

Library of Congress Cataloging-in-Publication Data

Holt, H. Barry
Digest of American Indian law : cases and chronology / H. Barry Holt, Gary Forrester.

p. cm.
Includes index.
ISBN 0-8377-0684-x
1. Indians of North America--Legal status, laws, etc.--Digests.
I. Forrester, Gary. II. Title.
KF8204.5.H65 1990
346.7301'3--dc20
[347.30613] 90-8491
CIP

Printed in the United States of America

ABOUT THE AUTHORS

H. Barry Holt received his A.B. degree from Occidental College in Los Angeles, an M.A. from Tulane University, and a Ph.D. from the University of Texas at Austin in Archeology and Social Anthropology. Dr. Holt served eight years as Regional Archeologist with the Bureau of Indian Affairs on the Navajo Reservation in Arizona and in the Pacific Northwest. He received his J.D. from the Northwestern School of Law of Lewis and Clark College, and he currently practices Environmental and Natural Resources Law in Phoenix, Arizona. Dr. Holt has lectured and written extensively on environmental and Indian law issues.

Gary Forrester holds B.A. and M.A. degrees from Eastern Illinois University, and he received his J.D. from the University of Illinois. He has extensive experience with Indian law, representing Indian tribes and individuals in South Dakota and as a former Director of the Native American Program at Oregon Legal Services, and serving as an adjunct Professor of Federal Indian Law at the Northwestern School of Law of Lewis and Clark College. Admitted to the practice of law in Australia, Mr. Forrester currently serves as an executive legal manager for the Accident Compensation Commission in Melbourne, Australia. He has written numerous articles on legal issues, including Australian Aboriginal Law and American Indian representation.

TABLE OF CONTENTS

PREFACE

Indian law is a unique, and misunderstood, area of the law. Arising out of a long history of confrontations between pioneers and settlers of European heritage and this country's native inhabitants, the tenets of Indian law reflect almost two hundred years of judicial struggle with a real clash of cultures.

Perhaps the most striking aspect of Indian law is its reliance on the history which gave it birth. While most lawsuits today involve applications of the common law or recent statutes in light of the latest precedents, lawsuits over Indian issues often devolve into interpretations of treaties negotiated over one hundred years ago. Testimony frequently consists of historical records of explorers or frontier leaders, along with anthropological evidence of historic or prehistoric native subsistence and settlement practices. This historic-anthropological gloss is only one of several characteristics of this complicated area of the law.

From the beginning of our country's judicial history, Indian tribes have been considered separate sovereigns, capable and entitled to self-government. However, almost all of the early history of Indian law seems to have focused on statutory, political, and philosophical limitations of that sovereignty. Federal power over Indians is constrained only by the United States Constitution. Yet today, the federal government seems to exercise that power less and less. Consequently, Indian tribes are developing sophisticated governments which increasingly challenge competing state governments. To all of this, add the antiquated concept of a federal trusteeship over dependent Indian wards, a concept which shows surprising vigor at selectively chosen moments, and there emerges one of the most complex and interesting areas of American law today.

As useful and revealing as are federal statutes pertaining to Indians, Indian law evolved and currently grows out of caselaw. It is for that reason that this *Digest* presents selected summaries of what we feel are the most important and revealing Indian law cases to date. This *Digest* is not intended to be used in a vacuum. Nothing can substitute for the detail and subtlety of the language of the judicial opinions themselves, the policies embodied in the numerous statutes pertaining to Indians, or the insights offered by many commentators on Indian affairs. Instead, it is intended as an easy-to-read and use sourcebook of the basic facts and holdings of cases important in the development of Indian law. We hope that the *Digest* will give lawyers, social scientists, students, and the interested public a guide to the cases, the keys which can open the door to this curious legal field.

The *Digest* begins with a brief chronological history of United States Indian policy since Columbus landed in the Americas. Historical events, important statutes, enunciated policies, and selected cases are intermixed to provide a backdrop for the case summaries that follow in the text. The cases are divided into three separate chapters by topic: The Federal-Indian Relationship, Jurisdiction, and Indian Reserved Rights. These chapters are then further divided into more specific sections and subsections within the general chapter topics.

Each case chapter, section, and subsection begins with a brief introductory essay, which identifies major litigation trends and summarizes the evolving state of the law in that area. The case summaries themselves are numbered and included in chronological order within the sections and subsections. It is in the nature of Indian law that one case may contain concepts essential to more than one topic. In those instances, each such case summary appears only once in the digest, within what we have selected as the most "important" topic to which the case contributes. The case is then referenced, by its name and primary topic location, in all other subsections to which it pertains.

Of necessity, we were limited in our selection of cases. As narrow as the field of Indian law is, there has been an enormous number of Indian cases decided over the last two hundred years, each of which provides some insight. We do feel, however, that the summaries of the particular cases we chose will allow the reader to discover and understand the general tenets of Indian law, and some of its subtleties, in a clear and interesting manner. To achieve that basic understanding is our primary goal.

I. CHRONOLOGY

A Brief History of Federal Indian Policy 1492-1989

1492 Columbus landed in the Americas. There were more years of legal contacts with American Indians before American Independence than there have been since.

1532 Franciscus de Victoria advised the King of Spain on the nature of aboriginal title. "The aborigines undoubtedly had true dominion in both public and private matters . . . neither their princes nor private persons could be despoiled of their property on the ground of their not being true owners." Spain could acquire title to Indian lands only through conquest in a "just war," or by obtaining title through the Indians' "free and voluntary choice" (i.e., treaties).

1630 "New Project of Freedoms and Exemptions" of the Dutch West India Company required the Company's officials to negotiate and purchase land from the Indian leaders of New Netherlands.

1636 The Rhode Island Plantations were founded by Roger Williams. He believed that English patents issued for colonization could not diminish Indian ownership of the land. He made treaties with the Narragansetts.

1651 In Rhode Island, agreements between Indians and individual colonists were forbidden.

1754 Benjamin Franklin proposed a union of colonies at the Albany Congress. A principal purpose was to assure centralizing control over Indian affairs.

1754-1763 During the French and Indian War, many Indian tribes sided with the French. The English Crown assumed responsibility for dealing with the Indians, rather than continuing to leave it to the individual colonies.

1763 In the Proclamation of 1763, the English King forbade the governors of the colonies to grant survey warrants or to issue patents on lands reserved for the Indians. Lands west of the

Appalachians were designated Indian territory. Even for lands east of the Appalachians, the Crown required licensing and approval of all transfers of Indian lands. British subjects on Indian lands were ordered to remove themselves.

1776 After the American Declaration of Independence, many Indian tribes sided with England in the War for Independence.

1778 The Treaty with the Delaware Tribe was the first treaty between the United States and an Indian tribe. The treaty guaranteed the territorial integrity of the Delaware Nation and anticipated that the Delawares might form a state and join the Confederation of States, along with other tribes.

1781 The Articles of Confederation were adopted, in which Article IX vested the Continental Congress with "the sole and exclusive right and power of . . . regulating the trade and managing all affairs with Indians not members of any of the states; provided, that the legislative right of any state within its own limits be not infringed or violated. . . ."

1784 The Treaty with the Six Nations was signed. The State of New York disrupted the federal negotiations and later negotiated its own treaties with the Six Nations that established conflicting boundary lines.

1785 The Treaty with the Cherokees (Hopewell) was signed. North Carolina protested that the federal negotiations violated states' rights by guaranteeing Cherokee lands within North Carolina and by providing that the Cherokees were under the protection of the United States and "no other sovereign."

1787 The Continental Congress passed the Northwest Ordinance: "The utmost good faith" shall be shown to the Indians; their property "shall never be taken from them without their consent"; and "they shall never be invaded or disturbed, unless in just and lawful wars authorized by Congress."

Georgia negotiated treaties with a group claiming to represent the Creeks, after the federal government had refused to deal with the group because it was unrepresentative of the Creeks. The Continental Congress refused to assist Georgia in the ensuing Indian war, on the grounds that the states lack the power to make war with the Indians or buy land from them.

1789 The United States Constitution was adopted. Article I, Section 8, Clause 3 authorized Congress to regulate "commerce . . . with the Indian tribes." Article II, Section 2, Clause 2 empowered the President to make treaties, including Indian treaties, with the consent of the Senate.

1790 The First Congress enacted the first Trade and Intercourse Act (now at 25 U.S.C. § 177). No sale of Indian lands was valid without United States authority. The Act was extended in 1793, 1796, 1802, 1817, 1822, and 1834. Whites were restricted on entering Indian country; Indian trade was regulated; liquor was prohibited from Indian country; federal standards were set governing crimes by one race against another; and "civilization and education" among the Indians was promoted.

1803 The Louisiana Purchase was consummated. This, together with the acquisition of Florida in 1812 to 1819, doubled the size of the United States. "Manifest destiny" was born.

1810 *Fletcher v. Peck.* This was the first Supreme Court case to address Indian law, and it held that the State held Indian lands within state borders in fee simple, subject to the Indian right of occupancy. Thus, the State could grant the land subject to Indian title.

1812-1815 The War of 1812 was fought. After the British withdrew from the continental United States, Indian tribes lost the power of allying with either the United States or the British. After 1815, treaty negotiations became more one-sided and treaties were used to accommodate westward expansion.

1817 The General Crimes Act (Federal Enclaves Act), 18 U.S.C. § 1152, provided for federal prosecution of federally defined crimes perpetrated by non-Indians against Indians in Indian country, and of non-major crimes perpetrated by Indians against non-Indians in Indian country. The Act did not apply to offenses by one Indian against another. This was the first statute providing for federal criminal jurisdiction over tribal Indians in Indian country.

1820-1861 This has been called the "Removal Period." Especially after 1828, when Andrew Jackson was elected president, federal Indian policy called for the removal of Indian tribes beyond state boundary lines. Tribes were removed from the Southeast, the Midwest, and the Pacific Northwest to the Indian Territory (Oklahoma, Kansas, and Arkansas).

1823 *Johnson v. McIntosh.* This case defined the Discovery Doctrine and the nature of Indian title: discovery gives title good against all other European nations, subject to the Indian right of occupancy, which the discoverer may extinguish by purchase or conquest.

1825 The Assimilated Crimes Act, 18 U.S.C. § 1111, incorporated state criminal law and applied it, through federal law, to areas under federal jurisdiction. Under the General Crimes Act of 1817, the Assimilated Crimes Act is applicable to Indian country.

1831 *Cherokee Nation v. Georgia.* This case established the guardian-ward principle (i.e., the trust relationship) between the United States and Indian tribes, and it coined the phrase "domestic dependent nation" to characterize tribes.

1832 *Worcester v. Georgia.* This decision found that state laws can have no force in Indian country.

1849 The Bureau of Indian Affairs was moved from the War Department to the Department of the Interior.

1861 The Enabling Act for the Kansas Territory contained the first clear congressional recognition that Indian reservations were intended as permanent jurisdictional enclaves within the states.

1865 Reservation schools were established under Christian organizations.

1871 Congress ended formal treaty-making with Indian tribes. Reservations after that time were established by statute or (until Congress ended the practice in 1919) by Executive Order of the President.

1878 Off-reservation boarding schools were established to permit education of Indian children away from the reservation environment.

1881 *United States v. McBratney.* The Supreme Court held that state law applies to a crime by a non-Indian against a non-Indian on an Indian reservation.

1883 *Ex Parte Crow Dog.* The murder of one Indian by another in Indian country was within the sole jurisdiction of the Indian Tribe; federal courts had no power over the case.

Courts of Indian Offenses were authorized under federal regulations, with judges to be appointed by the Indian agents. The Code of Indian Offenses, which the courts implemented, outlawed many traditional Indian cultural practices.

1884 *Elk v. Wilkins.* This case held that an Indian was not made a citizen by the Fourteenth Amendment to the Constitution, even though he was living apart from his tribe. The Court also ruled that general acts of Congress are not usually applicable to Indians unless there is a clear indication that Indians were meant to have been included.

1885 The Major Crimes Act, 18 U.S.C. § 1153, provided for federal court jurisdiction over seven major crimes committed by Indians on reservations against another Indian. The list was later expanded to fourteen enumerated crimes.

1886 *United States v. Kagama.* The Supreme Court upheld the Major Crimes Act, based on the federal government's trust responsibility to Indians. The Court declared that "the people of the states . . . are often [the Indians'] deadliest enemies."

1887 The General Allotment Act (Dawes Act), 25 U.S.C. § 31 *et seq,* provided for dividing the reservations into separate parcels, to encourage individual Indians in agricultural pursuits (160 acres per family, 80 acres per single person). Any land left over after allotment was declared surplus and opened up for settlement by non-Indians. Title to the Indian allotments was to be held in trust by the United States for 25 years, after which time title was to be conveyed to the Indian allottee in fee. The Indian allottees were to become United States citizens, subject to state criminal and civil law. Under the Act, Indian-held lands declined from 138 million acres in 1887 to 48 million in 1934, 20 million of which was desert.

1890 An attempt to suppress the Ghost Dance Religion led to the massacre of 146 Indians at Wounded Knee, South Dakota. The Indian Wars on the plains drew to a close.

1891 The leasing program for Indian lands began, pursuant to a federal statute. The Secretary of the Interior could lease allotted lands whenever he found that the allottee was unable to improve and occupy the allotment. Tribal lands could also be leased by the tribal council, subject to the Secretary's approval.

1895 *Talton v. Mayes.* This case held that the Bill of Rights applied only to the federal government or (through the Fourteenth Amendment) to the states, but not to tribal governments.

1903 *Lone Wolf v. Hitchcock.* This case established the "trust relationship" as a source of federal power (the "plenary power" over Indian affairs). Congress could abrogate previously established treaty rights with a later statute.

1905 *United States v. Winans.* The Supreme Court held that a treaty may reserve a tribe's right to hunt or fish off-reservation "at usual and accustomed places." Also, a treaty "is not a grant of rights to the Indians, but a grant of rights from them--a reservation of those not granted."

1908 *Winters v. United States.* This case was the source of the "Winters Doctrine": when Indian reservations are established, there is an implied reservation of enough water to effectuate the purposes of the reservation. These water rights are not based upon prior appropriation, nor upon actual beneficial use. The *Winters* rights are superior to all appropriations after the establishment of the reservation, and they are not forfeited if not used.

1913 *United States v. Sandoval.* Even though New Mexico Indian Pueblos held their land in fee simple under Spanish land grants, the Supreme Court held that Pueblo lands were Indian country. Consequently, a federal prohibition against liquor in Indian Country extended to the Pueblo lands, based upon the trust relationship with the Pueblo Indians.

1916 *United States v. Nice.* The Supreme Court concluded that United States citizenship for Indians "is not incompatible with tribal existence or continued guardianship," and may be conferred without placing Indians beyond the reach of congressional regulations adopted for the Indians' protection.

1921 The Snyder Act, 25 U.S.C. § 13, authorized the Bureau of Indian Affairs to expend congressionally appropriated moneys for "the benefit, care and assistance of the Indians throughout the United States," for health, education, economic development, and other purposes.

1924 United States citizenship was conferred upon all Indians "born within the territorial limits of the United States."

1928 The Merriam Report summarized the failures of federal Indian policies since the late nineteenth century.

1934 The Indian Reorganization Act, 25 U.S.C. §§ 461, provided for an end to the allotment system, encouraged tribal self-government through tribal constitutions, protected and expanded tribal land bases, and established Indian preference in hiring within the Bureau of Indian Affairs.

The Johnson-O'Malley Act, 25 U.S.C. §§452-457, encouraged enrollment of Indian children in state-controlled schools by reimbursing states for the cost of educating Indian children who came from tax-exempt Indian lands.

1935 *United States v. Creek Nation.* This case held that recognized Indian treaty lands taken from the Creeks and sold by the federal government, due to a surveying error, gave rise to Fifth Amendment compensation from the government, under the trust responsibility.

1938 *United States v. Shoshone Tribe.* This case found that a tribe's right of occupancy included the timber and mineral resources on the reservation, at least where title is "recognized." Consequently, the taking of those rights by the government was compensable under the Fifth Amendment.

1942 *Sioux Tribe v. United States.* The Supreme Court held that lands set aside for Indian reservations by executive order, rather than by treaty or statute, may be taken by the federal government without compensation.

Seminole Nation v. United States. The case confirmed that the government was more than a contracting party when it entered into a treaty with Indians--it was to be judged by "the most exacting fiduciary standards." Consequently, the United States was liable when funds were delivered to the tribal government, which was known to be defrauding its members.

1946 After dealing with Indian claims for compensation through 142 ad hoc jurisdictional statutes for nearly a century, Congress created the Indian Claims Commission, 25 U.S.C. § 70. The Commission expired in 1978, and the remaining 102 unresolved dockets were transferred to the United States Court of Claims.

1948 "Indian country" was defined, in 18 U.S.C. § 1151, as all land within an Indian reservation (including rights-of-way), all "dependent Indian communities," and all Indian allotments still held in trust by the government. This statute specifically applies only to criminal cases, but the Supreme Court has since extended this definition of Indian country to include all civil cases.

1949 The Hoover Commission issued a report on Indian affairs, calling for the total assimilation of Indians "into the mass of the population as full, tax-paying citizens."

1952 The McCarran Water Rights Suit Act (McCarran Amendment), 43 U.S.C. § 666, waived United States sovereign immunity in water rights adjudications, encouraged state adjudication proceedings, and provided that all water users would be bound by state adjudication. The McCarran Amendment applies to both federal and Indian reserved water rights.

1953 In House Concurrent Resolution 108, Congress adopted the Termination Policy, stating the aim "as rapidly as possible, to make the Indians within the territorial limits of the United States subject to the same laws and entitled to the same privileges and responsibilities as are applicable to other citizens of the United States, [and] to end their status as wards of the United States."

Public Law 280 (18 U.S.C. §§ 1161-62, 25 U.S.C. §§ 1321-22, 28 U.S.C. § 1360) extended state civil and criminal jurisdiction to Indian country in California, Nebraska, Minnesota (except Red Lake Reservation), Oregon (except Warm Springs Reservation), and Wisconsin. Alaska was added to the list when it was admitted to statehood in 1958. P.L. 280 also provided that any other state could assume such jurisdiction by statute or state constitutional amendment.

1954-1966 Congress enacted separate statutes terminating the federal relationship with 109 Indian tribes and bands. More than 11,400 individuals lost their status as "recognized" Indians, and approximately 1.5 million acres of Indian land were removed from protected trust status. The Bureau of Indian Affairs implemented a "relocation" program to encourage Indians to leave reservation areas and move to metropolitan areas.

1955 *Tee-Hit-Ton Indians v. United States.* This case held that the federal government will only be liable under the Fifth Amendment for takings of Indian title recognized by Congress in a treaty or statute, rather than original Indian title.

1956 *Squire v. Capoeman.* The Supreme Court determined that income or capital gains derived directly from allotted lands cannot be subjected to federal taxation, while the lands are held in trust for the Indian owner by the United States.

1959 *Williams v. Lee.* This case held that state courts have no subject matter jurisdiction over a civil claim by a non-Indian against an Indian for a transaction arising on a reservation, since that would infringe on tribal self-government.

1963 *Arizona v. California (I).* The Court found that water rights, necessary to make reservation land habitable and productive, were reserved under the Winters doctrine as of the time of the creation of the reservations. The tribes were entitled to enough water to irrigate all the "practicably irrigable acreage" on the reservations.

1965 *Warren Trading Post v. Arizona Tax Commission.* Since on-reservation trading posts were federally licensed and subject to extensive federal regulation, the Supreme Court found that state laws were preempted and Arizona could not tax the gross receipts of a non-Indian operated trading post.

1966 Congress, in 28 U.S.C. § 1362, authorized any Indian tribe to file suit in federal district court, without reference to the amount in controversy, for cases arising under federal law (jurisdictional statute).

1968 The Indian Civil Rights Act, 25 U.S.C. § 1301 *et seq.*, required Indian tribes to observe most of the guarantees of the United States Bill of Rights. It authorized federal court habeas corpus jurisdiction to review tribal convictions, and provided for retrocession of P.L. 280 jurisdiction.

Menominee Tribe v. United States. This case held that termination did not abrogate the Tribe's treaty hunting and fishing rights, because the Menominee Termination Act contained no clear statement of congressional intent to abrogate those rights. Thus, Wisconsin could not enforce state game and fish licensing and regulatory laws against tribal members.

Puyallup Tribe v. Department of Game (Puyallup I). This decision permitted some state regulation of off-reservation treaty fishing rights, in the interests of conservation, "provided the regulation meets appropriate standards and does not discriminate against the Indians."

1970 President Nixon's message to Congress ended the Termination Era and inaugurated an era of tribal "self-determination," strengthening tribal sovereignty and advocating protection of the Indian land base and economic resources.

Federal Power Commission v. Tuscarora Indian Nation. The Supreme Court held that "general Acts of Congress apply to Indians as well as to all others in the absence of a clear expression to the contrary." Thus, the Federal Power Act, which provided for the condemnation of lands needed for a project, applied to fee-owned lands of the Tribe despite an exception for Indian reservations, because the Tuscaroras had no treaty or trust land.

Choctaw Nation v. Oklahoma. The case held that the establishment of a reservation included the bed of a navigable water on the reservation, in view of the government's specific promises in the treaty that the tribal lands would never be part of any state or territory.

1971 The Alaska Native Claims Settlement Act, 43 U.S.C. § 1601 *et seq.*, extinguished native title to the land (including submerged lands and hunting and fishing rights). In return, Alaskan natives received fee title to over 40 million acres of land, federal payments of $462.5 million over an eleven-year period, and a 2 percent royalty on mineral development in Alaska (limited to $500 million). The Act also organized Alaskan natives into thirteen regional corporations and various village corporations, which received corporate stock and selected lands.

1972 The Indian Education Act, 20 U.S.C. § 887c, gave Indian parents increased control over federal funds made available to public schools, to be used for Indian education needs.

1973 *McClanahan v. Arizona State Tax Commission.* This case clarified the holding of *Williams v. Lee,* concluding that when only Indians or Indian interests are involved, state power (e.g., to impose an income tax) is usually excluded unless federal statutes or treaties confer it. When a case involves non-Indian parties, the *Williams v. Lee* infringement test will be applied to determine whether a state may assert jurisdiction over a matter arising in Indian country. *McClanahan* first articulated the federal "preemption" test, to be applied against the "backdrop" of historical tribal sovereignty.

1973-1986 Congress enacted separate statutes restoring the federal relationship with previously terminated Indian tribes. The Menominee Tribe became the first "terminated tribe" to be restored, with their lands placed back into trust. Through 1986, ten tribes had been restored to their former status.

1974 The Indian Financing Act, 25 U.S.C. § 1451, established a federal revolving loan fund for Indian economic development and provided federal loan guarantees for private sector loans to support such development.

Morton v. Mancari. The Supreme Court upheld a statutory "Indian preference" for hiring by the Bureau of Indian Affairs. This was not an impermissible racial classification, but a political preference based upon the government-to-government relationship between Indian tribes and the United States.

Morton v. Ruiz. This case held that in the absence of properly promulgated Bureau of Indian Affairs rules limiting general assistance benefits to "on-reservation" Indians, an Indian living near the reservation was also entitled to such benefits pursuant to the Snyder Act of 1921.

1975 The Indian Self-Determination and Education Assistance Act (P.L. 93-638), 25 U.S.C. § 450 *et seq.,* strengthened tribal governmental control over federally funded programs for Indians, including programs for educational assistance to local school districts. The Secretaries of the Interior and Health and Human Services were authorized to contract with Indian tribes for federally funded programs, under which the tribes themselves assumed responsibility for administering the federal programs.

The American Indian Policy Review Commission was established by Congress to undertake a comprehensive review of federal Indian policy and to consider alternative methods for strengthening tribal government. The Commission's report, issued in 1977, called for reaffirmation of the status of tribes as self-governing institutions and a rejection of assimilationist policies.

United States v. Mazurie. The Supreme Court held that federal legislation, delegating to Indian tribes the authority to regulate liquor in Indian country, was valid even as applied to non-Indians. Although such a delegation to a "private, voluntary association" would be invalid, the tribes, as sovereigns, already possessed some independent regulatory authority over the subject matter.

De Coteau v. District County Court. An 1891 Act, opening the Lake Traverse Reservation for homesteading, was held to have terminated the reservation, even though the Act made no mention of changing reservation boundaries. The Supreme Court relied heavily on the "legislative history and surrounding circumstances," including newspaper accounts, in reaching its decision. In passing, the Court observed that 18 U.S.C. § 1151 defines Indian country for civil as well as criminal cases.

1976 The Indian Health Care Improvement Act was enacted, 25 U.S.C. § 1601 *et seq.*, reflecting the federal government's trust responsibility to provide economic and social services necessary to ensure a standard of living for Indians comparable to non-Indian society.

Moe v. Confederated Salish and Kootenai Tribes. The Supreme Court permitted the state to impose a tax on cigarette sales by an Indian seller to a non-Indian purchaser in Indian country. The Indian seller was required to collect the tax and turn it over to the state. The tax itself fell on the non-Indian purchaser.

Bryan v. Itasca County. This case held that P.L. 280 did not authorize a state property tax against personal property owned by an Indian in Indian country, even though the state had been granted civil jurisdiction. Thus, P.L. 280 grants adjudicatory jurisdiction only; it does not subject tribes to "the full panoply of civil regulatory powers of state and local governments."

Fisher v. District Court. The Supreme Court applied the Williams v. Lee infringement test to a state court adoption proceeding, even though only Indians were involved. The Supreme Court concluded that state jurisdiction would interfere with tribal self-government, and that the tribal court's exclusive jurisdiction derived not from the race of the parties but from the Tribe's quasi-sovereign status.

Colorado River Water Conservation District v. United States. The Supreme Court held that the McCarren Amendment (by which the United States consented to suit in state court in water disputes) applied to suits involving reserved Indian water rights, where the United States is the named defendant as trustee. In such state court actions, the nature and extent of reserved Indian water rights remain matters of federal law. Although federal courts retain concurrent jurisdiction with the states in these cases, "wise judicial administration" requires that the federal court defer to the state courts in the absence of substantive proceedings in federal court.

1977 *Rosebud Sioux Tribe v. Kneip.* The Supreme Court found that Congress had diminished the Rosebud Sioux Reservation through acts opening the reservation to white settlement, even though the acts made no mention of changing reservation boundaries. The Court relied on the "surrounding circumstances and legislative history" to determine congressional intent.

1978 The Indian Child Welfare Act, 25 U.S.C. § 1901 *et seq.*, established "minimum Federal standards for the removal of Indian children from their families and the placement of such children in foster or adoptive homes which will reflect the unique values of Indian culture." Tribal courts were granted extensive jurisdiction in implementing the Act.

Santa Clara Pueblo v. Martinez. This case upheld tribal sovereign immunity from suit, and held that habeas corpus was the sole remedy for enforcement of the Indian Civil Rights Act in federal court. Violations of the Indian Civil Rights Act which do not involve detention by the tribe must be remedied in tribal courts.

Oliphant v. Suquamish Tribe. The Supreme Court found that tribes have no general criminal jurisdiction over non-Indians. The Court held that such jurisdiction is inconsistent with the status of tribes as dependent sovereigns.

United States v. Wheeler. This case held that the Fifth Amendment's bar against double jeopardy was not violated when an Indian was convicted in federal court after having been convicted of a lesser included offense in tribal court. The tribe has inherent criminal jurisdiction over its members; such jurisdiction does not derive from the federal government.

The American Indian Religious Freedom Act, 42 U.S.C. § 1996, declared the United States policy of protecting the exercise of traditional Native American religions.

The Bureau of Indian Affairs established criteria, in 25 C.F.R. § 54, for determining which unrecognized tribes are entitled to be federally acknowledged as tribes. Some 100 groups fell into the "unrecognized" category in 1977.

1979 *Washington v. Confederated Bands and Tribes of the Yakima Nation.* The Supreme Court held that P.L. 280 authorized a state to assume selective geographic and subject matter jurisdiction over Indian country, if that is what the state chose to do. Although state legislation (unlike federal legislation) may not generally single out Indians for special treatment, this singling out was permissible within the context of P.L. 280.

Washington v. Washington State Commercial Passenger Fishing Vessel Association. This case established the proposition that Indians are entitled, under treaties reserving "the right of taking fish . . . in common with all citizens of the territory," to take up to 50 percent of the harvestable anadromous fish run. The State may set catch limits, but only as needed for conservation.

1980 *United States v. Mitchell (I).* The Supreme Court held that the limited trust relationship created under the General Allotment Act did not give rise to a claim for damages against the United States for mismanagement of the Tribe's timber resources.

White Mountain Apache Tribe v. Bracker. This case determined that a state motor carrier license tax (based on gross receipts) and a state fuel use tax were preempted by federal law from applying to non-Indian contractors cutting timber on the reservation for delivery to the tribal sawmill. The federal government had regulated extensively timber operations in Indian country.

United States v. Sioux Nation. The Supreme Court held that an 1877 Act of Congress ceding the Black Hills was a "taking" within the meaning of the Fifth Amendment, thereby entitling the Tribe to compensation of $17.5 million plus approximately $100 million in interest. The plenary authority of Congress established under *Lone Wolf* is "subject to limitations inhering in . . . a guardianship and to pertinent constitutional restrictions."

The Maine Indian Claims Settlement Act, 25 U.S.C. § 1721 *et. seq.*, extinguished original Indian title and provided federal funds for purchase of lands for the tribes. The Act arose out of litigation which upheld the tribes' claims to aboriginal title because the lands had not been conveyed with federal approval.

1981 *Montana v. United States.* This case held that the State owned the bed of the Big Horn River despite the 1868 Treaty which reserved the land through which the river ran to the Tribe. The rule that the federal government holds lands under navigable waters for future states overcame both the rule that treaties are to be construed in favor of the Indians and that the treaties are grants from, not to, the Indians. The Supreme Court also held that the Tribe cannot regulated non-Indian hunting and fishing on non-Indian lands on the reservation.

1982 *Merrion v. Jicarilla Apache Tribe.* The Supreme Court held that tribes organized under the Indian Reorganization Act have the inherent authority to impose severance taxes on mineral development of tribal resources by non-Indian lessees, even though the leases did not provide for such taxation. The power to tax is "an essential attribute of Indian sovereignty."

The Indian Mineral Development Act, 25 U.S.C. § 2101 *et seq.*, provided encouragement for Indian tribes to develop their own mineral resources.

1983 President Reagan's American Indian Policy committed the United States to a government-to-government relationship with recognized Indian tribes. It emphasized the need for tribes to become self-sufficient by reducing their dependence on federal funding and increasing their role in the development of reservation economies.

The Indian Tribal Governmental Tax Status Act, 26 U.S.C. § 7871, granted a deduction from federal income tax for taxes paid to a tribal government. It also provided that charitable contributions to Indian tribal governments are deductions for federal income, estate, and gift tax purposes. Indian tribal governments were exempted from a variety of excise taxes, and certain governmental obligations issued by Indian tribal governments were provided an income tax exemption.

Rice v. Rehner. This case held that in the area of liquor sales by a licensed Indian trader to non-members of the Tribe for off-premises consumption, states are not preempted from regulating, despite heavy federal involvement in the field. The off-reservation impact justifies state intervention.

United States v. Mitchell (II). The Supreme Court found that the Tucker Act (which authorized Court of Claims jurisdiction over the United States for certain claims) is a waiver of sovereign immunity. Consequently, the Tribe can sue the United States for mismanagement of the Tribe's timber resources in violation of various federal statutes and regulations which establish a fiduciary duty.

Arizona v. California (II). The Supreme Court held that the tribes could not reopen the question of "practically irrigable acreage" in determining *Winters* rights, even though the tribes claimed that omitted lands within reservation boundaries resulted in a 15 to 22 percent error in previous litigation. The

Court stressed the "need for certainty in the holding and use of water rights." The Court also found that the tribes can intervene as "independent qualified members of the modern body politic"--they do not have to rely upon United States representation. Also, the United States had not had a conflict of interest in representing the tribes despite the presence of conflicting federal rights.

New Mexico v. Mescalero Apache Tribe. In view of the Tribe's extensive management program and the independence of tribal fishing and hunting programs from the State, the Supreme Court found that the State could not enforce its hunting and fishing laws against any person, Indian or non-Indian, within the reservation. Extensive federal assistance, and the fact that almost the entire reservation was tribally owned, were important factors justifying preemption of state law.

1984 *Three Affiliated Tribes v. Wold Engineering.* This court found that the Tribe could bring a civil action in state court against a non-Indian, despite the lack of P.L. 280 jurisdiction. P.L. 280 did not divest state courts of preexisting jurisdiction. Tribal self-government is not impeded when a state allows an Indian to seek relief against a non-Indian concerning a claim arising in Indian country.

Escondido Mutual Water Co. v. La Jolla . . . Bands. This case determined that under the Federal Power Act (FPA), hydroelectric project licenses could be issued by the Federal Energy Regulatory Commission for on-reservation projects without the Tribe's consent. Tribal authority "to prevent a federal agency from carrying out its statutory responsibility . . . would seem to be inconsistent with [the Tribe's] status." Moreover, the FPA was intended to be applied to reservation lands without tribal consent.

The Report of the Presidential Commission on Indian Reservation Economies identified weak tribal business management and unstable tribal governments, Bureau of Indian Affairs financial inflexibility and failure to inventory and manage tribal resources, and jurisdictional disputes with local governments as major obstacles to reservation economic development. The Commission recommended creation of a new federal trust agency to administer block grants to tribes and protect Indian resources. In addition, the Commission encouraged modernization of tribal governments, limited federal judicial review of tribal court decisions, and reservation-wide referenda on jurisdictional matters.

1985 *Kerr-McGee Corp. v. Navajo Tribe.* The Supreme Court found that the Tribe, which did not adopt the Indian Reorganization Act and had no requirement that the Secretary of Interior approve taxation ordinances, had the inherent sovereign power to tax members and non-members. The Secretary's regulation of mining leases on tribal land did not include review of tribal taxes on mineral production.

National Farmer's Insurance Co. v. Crow Tribe. The Supreme Court held that tribal court is the appropriate forum for determining whether the Tribe has jurisdiction over a civil suit involving a non-Indian and an Indian on non-Indian land within the reservation. Once tribal remedies are exhausted, however, "a federal court may determine . . . whether a tribal court has exceeded the lawful limits of its jurisdiction."

Oregon Department of Fish and Wildlife v. Klamath Tribe. This case determined that when the Tribe ceded "all their claim, right, title, and interest in and to" a portion of their reservation, the reservation was diminished. Since the Tribe's hunting and fishing rights were limited to within the boundaries of the reservation, those rights no longer exist in the ceded area.

1986 *United States v. Dion.* The Supreme Court found that when Congress amended the Bald Eagle Act in 1962 to include provisions for Indians' taking of eagles for religious purposes, it was a clear indication that Congress "believed that it was abrogating the rights of Indians to take eagles." Since the right to take eagles was abrogated, there can be no treaty right defense against prosecution for killing a bald eagle under the Endangered Species Act.

United States v. White Mountain Apache Tribe. This case held that the sovereign power of Indian tribes to exclude non-members from the reservation does not extend to federal agents or employees performing official duties. Any such attempted exclusion is barred by the sovereign immunity of the United States, despite tribal charges of improper conduct of official business.

United States v. Eberhardt. The court found that the statutory authority of the Department of the Interior to supervise and manage Indian affairs and property authorized the Department to regulate tribal fishing on the reservation for the benefit of the Indians.

1987 *Iowa Mutual Insurance Co. v. LaPlante.* The Supreme Court held that when a dispute is pending before an Indian tribal court, the federal courts may not exercise diversity jurisdiction before the tribal court system has had the opportunity to determine its own jurisdiction.

California v. Cabazon Band of Mission Indians. The Supreme Court found that P.L. 280, under which the State of California was granted civil and criminal jurisdiction over Indian lands within its borders, did not authorize the State to apply state and county gambling laws to Indian reservation bingo and card game gambling where the state and county laws regulated rather than prohibited gambling.

1988 *Lyng v. Northwest Indian Cemetery Protective Association.* The Supreme Court held that the First Amendment did not give any citizens, including Native Americans, the right to veto public programs that do not prohibit the free exercise of religion. Further, the American Indian Religious Freedom Act does not create a cause of action or any judicially enforceable individual rights.

The Indian Self-Determination and Education Assistance Act Amendments of 1988 were passed by Congress to reduce bureaucratic and funding difficulties encountered by Indian tribes that attempted to contract with the United States to provide federal program services under the original Act of 1975. The Amendments require the Secretary of the Interior to approve tribal proposals for Self-Determination Act contracts within ninety days of receiving an application unless specific findings are made which justify declining the contract. In addition, the Amendments prohibit reducing available contract funds to pay for federal contract monitoring or to pay for costs of displaced federal personnel. Funds must also be made available for tribal indirect costs.

1989 *Oklahoma Tax Commission v. Graham.* The Supreme Court held that the possible existence of a tribal claim of sovereign immunity in a state tax claim case filed in state court did not convert the claims into federal questions which would provide a basis for removal to federal court.

Wyoming v. United States. The Supreme Court upheld, per curiam by an equally divided court, the Wyoming Supreme Court's general adjudication of all rights to use water in the Big Horn River System. In doing so, the Court upheld the "practicably irrigable acreage" standard for quantifying Indian reserved water rights.

Brendale v. Confederated Tribes and Bands of Yakima Indian Nation. In this case, the Supreme Court revealed its strong internal disagreements over the power of Indian tribes to regulate land use on reservations which contain non-Indian fee land. Three separate opinions resulted in a decision upholding tribal land use regulation of activities on fee land within a predominantly tribally owned portion of the reservation, and disallowing tribal land use regulation of activities on fee land in an area of the reservation substantially owned and occupied by non-tribal members and non-Indians.

1990 *Employment Division v. Smith.* With this decision, the Supreme Court further limited Indian religious practices, holding that states can incidentally prohibit the religious use of peyote so long as the prohibition is generally applicable and not specifically directed toward prohibiting the exercise of religion.

Duro v. Reina. The Supreme Court held that an Indian tribal court had no criminal jurisdiction over a non-member Indian who killed another non-member Indian on the reservation.

II. THE FEDERAL - INDIAN RELATIONSHIP

There have been over two hundred years of historical dealings between the United States and Indian tribes. During that time, federal policies toward Indians have changed, sometimes radically. Several aspects of the federal-Indian relationship, however, reflect its nature and can be consistently traced throughout this history.

Indian tribes as governments occupy a unique position in our governmental system. They are separate political entities, to which the United States Constitution does not apply. But despite their sovereignty, Indian tribes still are subject to the plenary power of Congress, with few limits to that power.

Although tribes function outside of constitutional restraints, general acts of Congress still apply to their members. The only exception to this is when a general law conflicts with specific privileges granted to the Indians by treaty or statute. Then, the general law applies only if Congress has manifested a specific intent to override the special privilege. Individual Indians, although bound by general laws, have fought for decades for the same constitutional protections applying to non-Indians. This is particularly evident with regard to cultural and religious matters.

The federal-Indian trust relationship defines the respective roles of the federal government and Indian tribes in their interactions. Despite tribal sovereignty, the trust beneficiary status afforded Indian tribes provides both benefits and limitations. The federal trust responsibility imposes duties of fair dealing and protection of Indian lands and resources on the United States. However, those duties also restrict Indian use of their property and proscribe tribal actions inconsistent with their dependent status.

Courts have become increasingly more specific regarding the relationships between Indians and the United States, and these relationships continue to evolve. Future litigation will provide even more insight into how Indians and the federal government will interact for years to come.

A. Governmental Relationship

Some of the earliest Supreme Court cases dealt with the legal nature of the Indian presence in the United States. *Johnson v. McIntosh* in 1823 defined Indian aboriginal title and, in its discussion of the Doctrine of Discovery, set the stage for all future dealings between the federal government and Indian tribes. Later decisions elaborated on the unique status of tribal governments. The *Cherokee Nation v. Georgia* decision in 1831 confirmed that Indian nations were distinct, self-governing political entities that were nonetheless dependent upon the United States as their guardian.

In 1832, the Supreme Court in *Worcester v. Georgia* held that state laws did not apply to Indian lands. In 1895, *Talton v. Mayes* found that since Indian governments did not derive from the United States Constitution, the Fifth Amendment did not apply to their actions. In a similar holding much later in 1959, the *Native American Church v. Navajo Tribal Council* court confirmed that the Constitution applies to tribal governmental actions only when the Constitution itself or Congress clearly indicates its applicability. This unique form of sovereignty became even more secure in 1978 when the Supreme Court in *Santa Clara Pueblo v. Martinez* determined that suits against Indian tribes were barred by sovereign immunity.

Despite the apparent independence of tribal governments, federal power over them has always been paramount. Some elements of this power arise from the duty, enunciated in 1886 in *United States v. Kagama*, of the United States to protect the tribes. Congress' power over Indians was first characterized as plenary in 1903 by the Supreme Court in *Lone Wolf v. Hitchcock*, which further described it as political power that is not subject to judicial review. While that power has been used to authorize expenditures for the benefit of Indians, it has also been used successfully to take Indian lands and property, subject to constitutional constraints, and even to determine tribal membership.

Recent cases emphasize the inability of Indian tribes to exercise power inconsistent with their dependent status. This even extends to congressionally authorized use of Indian lands without tribal consent. Most recently, the Ninth Circuit Court of Appeals in *United States v. White Mountain Apache Tribe* clearly stated that Indian tribes cannot interfere with congressionally mandated activities. Although tribes long have been held to retain sovereign powers, as tribes continue to exercise those powers they will increasingly conflict with the plenary power of Congress to control them.

1. *Fletcher v. Peck,* 10 U.S. (6 Cran.) 87 (1810).

Facts: Georgia invalidated certain land grants made under a previous statute. The purchaser under the original grants claimed title. The subsequent purchasers argued, inter alia, that Georgia never had the power to make the original grants since the land was subject to aboriginal Indian title.

Issue: Did Indian title prevent Georgia from holding fee simple title to the land?

Held: Georgia did hold the land in fee, despite Indian title recognized in the King's proclamation of 1763. "The nature of Indian title, which is certainly to be respected by all courts until it be legitimately extinguished, is not such as to be absolutely repugnant to seisin in fee on the part of the state." So Georgia had the power to grant the land. The Indians' interest is characterized as a right of occupancy, or right of soil. Georgia's fee came from a U.S. Commission.

Dissent: Justice Johnson wrote that Georgia did not have a fee simple in the property, but only a "mere possibility." The Indians in fact are the "absolute proprietors," and the restrictions upon their right of soil amount only to an exclusion of all competitors from their markets.

2. *Johnson v. McIntosh,* 21 U.S. (8 Wheat.) 543 (1823).

Facts: Certain "chiefs" of the Illinois and Piankeshaw tribes conveyed land to plaintiffs, private individuals.

Issue: Was the conveyance valid? What title did plaintiffs acquire?

Held: (1) Discovery doctrine: "discovery" gives title against all other European nations. That title may be consummated by possession.

(2) Indian right of occupancy: after discovery, Indians were still recognized as the rightful occupants of the soil, with a legal as well as just claim to retain possession of it. The title of the "discoverers" was subject to the Indian right of occupancy.

(3) Discovery gave the exclusive right to extinguish the Indian title of occupancy, "either by purchase or by conquest," to the discovering government.

(4) So, the plaintiffs acquired only the "Indian title of occupancy," not a title which can be sustained in the courts of the United States.

3. *Cherokee Nation v. Georgia*, 30 U.S. (5 Pet.) 1 (1831).

Facts: Cherokees sought an injunction to stop Georgia from enforcing state laws in Cherokee territory and from taking over Cherokee lands.

Issue: Does the Supreme Court have original jurisdiction in this case? Article III, Section 2 of the Constitution extends its judicial power to controversies "between a state or citizens thereof, and foreign states, citizens or subjects." Is the Cherokee Nation a "foreign state"?

Held: (1) The Cherokee Nation is a "state," a distinct political society, governing itself, and making treaties with the United States.

(2) But, the Cherokee Nation is not a "foreign" state. Indian tribes within the boundaries of the United States are "domestic dependent nations."

(3) Indian tribes "are in a state of pupilage; their relation to the United States resembles that of a ward to his guardian."

(4) In Article III, Section 8 (the Commerce Clause), foreign nations and Indian tribes are clearly distinguished.

(5) So, the Supreme Court has no original jurisdiction over this case.

4. *Worcester v. Georgia*, 31 U.S. (6 Pet.) 515 (1832).

Facts: Georgia enacted laws in 1830 requiring any person residing within the Cherokee Nation to have a license from the state governor. Worcester was prosecuted in state court for violating this law. Worcester was a missionary, licensed under the Federal Trade and Intercourse Acts.

Issue: Does Georgia have jurisdiction over the territory of the Cherokee Nation?

Held: (1) "[T]he language used in treaties with the Indians should never be construed to their prejudice."

(2) Indian nations are distinct, independent political communities, "possessors of the soil, from time immemorial." The only exception is that imposed by the Discovery Doctrine--that the tribes could deal only with the discoverer.

(3) "The laws of Georgia can have no force" in Cherokee territory, and the citizens of Georgia have no right to enter Cherokee territory without the Cherokees' consent or in conformity with federal law.

(4) The laws of Georgia were "repugnant to the Constitution, laws and treaties of the United States," and therefore null and void.

Concur: Justice McLean wrote that the exercise of the power of self-government by the Indians is "undoubtedly contemplated to be temporary." If a tribe loses the power of self-government "by moral degradation or a reduction of their numbers," then state law may be extended to them.

5. *United States v. Kagama,* 118 U.S. 375 (1886).

Facts: Two Indians were indicted under the Major Crimes Act for murdering another Indian on the reservation.

Issue: Was the Major Crimes Act outside Congress' power?

Held: (1) The Major Crimes Act does not cover "commerce," so it is not authorized by the Indian Commerce Clause.

(2) But, the "Indian tribes are the wards of the nation. They are communities dependent on the United States. . . . Because of local ill feeling, the people of the States where they are found are often their deadliest enemies." From this relationship arises the "duty of protection, and with it the power." Thus, the Act was a valid exercise of congressional power.

6. *Talton v. Mayes,* 163 U.S. 376 (1895).

Facts: An Indian was tried in tribal court for murder of another Indian in Indian country. The defendant challenged the grand jury composition as defective under the Fifth Amendment.

Issue: Do Cherokee laws derive from the Constitution of the United States, or do they have their own origin? Are Cherokee laws federal laws?

Held: The Fifth Amendment does not apply to the local laws of the Cherokees, because the Cherokees' powers of local government are "not created by the Constitution, although subject to its general provisions and the paramount authority of Congress."

7. *Lone Wolf v. Hitchcock,* 187 U.S. 553 (1903).

Facts: An 1867 treaty required that no further cession of Indian lands would take place without the approval of three-fourths of the adult males. In 1892, Congress passed an act which took additional lands, without the required consent.

Issue: Can the 1867 treaty be abrogated by a later federal statute which does not comply with the terms of the treaty?

Held: (1) Congress has plenary authority over the tribes, and the power is a political one, not subject to judicial review.

(2) Congress has the power to abrogate Indian treaties, just as it may abrogate a treaty with a foreign nation, if "consistent with perfect good faith towards the Indians."

8. *United States v. Sandoval,* 231 U.S. 28 (1913).

Facts: Congress prohibited the introduction of liquor into the Pueblo lands in New Mexico, which were owned in fee simple.

Issue: Were the Pueblo lands Indian country?

Held: (1) The Pueblos had been "regarded and treated by the United States as requiring special consideration and protection, like other Indian Communities."

(2) The extent of the guardianship relationship is to be determined by Congress, not the courts, so long as Congress has not arbitrarily "determined that a group is an Indian tribe."

(3) Thus, Congress can prohibit liquor into the Pueblo lands on the basis of the federal-Indian trust relationship as well as the Indian Commerce Clause, despite the Pueblos' citizenship and despite their fee simple title.

9. *United States v. Creek Nation,* 295 U.S. 103 (1935).

Facts: By treaty in 1833, the United States conveyed in fee and guaranteed quiet title in land in Indian Territory to the Creek Tribe. Through a series of survey errors, over 5,000 acres of this land was mistakenly allotted and patented to Sac and Fox Indians. The government, acknowledging the error, asserted that it was liable only for damages for the error.

Issue: Was the mistaken allotment and patenting of Creek land an appropriation by the government, entitling the Tribe to just compensation?

Held: (1) Although the Tribe might have been able to stop the land disposals at the time, "[i]t was in a state of tutelage and entitled to rely on the United States, its guardian, for needed protection of its interests."

(2) "We conclude that the lands were appropriated by the United States in circumstances which involved an implied undertaking by it to make just compensation to the tribe." The compensation should include the land value at the time of the taking, plus a reasonable rate of interest.

10. *Native American Church v. Navajo Tribal Council,* 272 F.2d 131 (10th Cir. 1959).

Facts: Tribal members, members of the Native American Church, were arrested and convicted in tribal court of violations of a tribal ordinance prohibiting the sale, use, and possession of peyote within Navajo country.

Issue: Does the tribal ordinance violate the Free Exercise of Religion Clause of the United States Constitution?

Held: (1) Indian nations have exclusive authority to govern their own internal affairs.

(2) "The First Amendment applies only to Congress. . . . It is made applicable to the States only by the Fourteenth Amendment. . . . But . . . Indian tribes are not states. They have a status higher than that of states."

(3) The Constitution "is binding upon Indian nations only where it expressly binds them, or is made binding by treaty or some act of Congress. No provision in the Constitution makes the First Amendment applicable to Indian nations nor is there any law of Congress doing so."

(4) "[N]either, under the Constitution or the laws of Congress, do the Federal courts have jurisdiction of tribal laws or regulations, even though they may have an impact to some extent on forms of religious worship."

11. *Seneca Nation of Indians v. Brucker (Seneca I),* 262 F.2d 27 (D.C. Cir. 1958), *cert. denied,* 360 U.S. 909 (1959).

Facts: The Allegheny River Project was designed to flood 10,000 acres of Seneca Nation lands, leaving less than 2,300 acres and forcing one-third of the population to leave the reservation.

Issue: Did Congress intend to flood Seneca lands?

Held: (1) Congress can authorize a taking by eminent domain despite treaty rights. "The question is whether Congress has, in a sufficiently clear and specific way, shown an intention to do so."

(2) Documents submitted to Congress regarding the project plainly showed that the project would flood Seneca lands, and debate over the authorizing legislation reveals an awareness of the taking of the land. "We think Congress has authorized the taking of these lands."

12. *Seneca Nation of Indians v. United States (Seneca II),* 338 F.2d 55 (2d Cir. 1964), *cert. denied,* 380 U.S. 952 (1965).

Facts: The Secretary of the Army proposed to relocate a highway in conjunction with the Allegheny River Project. The relocated highway would divide the remaining Seneca Nation lands in two.

Issue: Did Congress properly delegate its authority to condemn Indian lands to the Secretary of the Army?

Held: (1) "The replacement or relocation of existing highways unquestionably is a part of the reservoir project authorized by Congress."

(2) "Congress need not itself specifically and expressly authorize by 'special enactment' each particular taking of Indian land, but can choose to delegate some of its authority to administrative offices and agencies." This action was a reasonable exercise of delegated authority.

13. *Simmons v. Eagle Seelatsee,* 244 F. Supp. 808 (E.D. Wash. 1965), *aff'd,* 384 U.S. 209 (1966).

Facts: Congress enacted a statute permitting only Yakimas who were quarter blood or more to take restricted Yakima lands by will or by inheritance.

Issue: Was there a "rational basis" for this classification?

Held: (1) Congress has plenary control over Indian tribal relations and property, even after Indians are made citizens.

(2) Congress has "the power to regulate and determine tribal membership." This power includes the power to "classify Indians according to the percentages of Indian blood."

(3) Thus, the statute had a rational basis and was not akin to racial discrimination.

14. *Scholder v. United States,* 428 F.2d 1123 (9th Cir.), *cert. denied,* 400 U.S. 942 (1970).

Facts: The Bureau of Indian Affairs agreed to assist a non-Indian by building an irrigation lateral canal on the non-Indian's property, as part of an irrigation project which supplied water to both Indian and non-Indian land. Similar requests for Bureau assistance by Indians had been denied.

Issue: Did the expenditure violate the Snyder Act, 25 U.S.C. § 13, which authorizes Bureau expenditures to improve Indian irrigation systems?

Held: (1) The United States, and the Bureau of Indian Affairs, are immune from this suit on the basis of sovereign immunity.

(2) The named officials have not acted outside the authority of the Snyder Act, because the expenditure will improve a project which benefits Indians.

(3) However, the Bureau's conduct "borders on the shocking" and reflects "gross insensitivity."

15. *Morton v. Ruiz,* 415 U.S. 199 (1973).

Facts: Plaintiff was a Papago Indian living fifteen miles off the reservation. When his union went on strike, he was denied welfare benefits by both the state and the Bureau of Indian Affairs. The Bureau's reason was that he did not live on the reservation.

Issue: Does the Snyder Act, 25 U.S.C. § 13, which authorizes the Bureau to provide services to Indians "throughout the United States," limit such services to on-reservation Indians?

Held: (1) The Secretary of the Interior can create reasonable eligibility requirements in order to allocate the limited funds available to him under the Snyder Act.

(2) But, even if the Secretary could limit "on or near" appropriations to only on-reservation Indians, the Bureau had not properly promulgated eligibility requirements which would have so limited the expenditures.

(3) Thus, plaintiff was entitled to benefits.

16. *Santa Clara Pueblo v. Martinez,* 436 U.S. 49 (1978).

Facts: The Tribe passed an ordinance denying tribal membership to children of female members who married outside the Tribe, while extending membership to children of male members who marry outside the Tribe.

Issue: Did the ordinance violate the equal protection provision of the Indian Civil Rights Act (ICRA)? Are the federal courts available in actions against the Tribe under the Indian Civil Rights Act?

Held: (1) "Suits against the tribe under the ICRA are barred by its sovereign immunity from suit."

(2) Tribal officers may be sued under the ICRA, but only in tribal forums. "Tribal courts have repeatedly been recognized as appropriate forums for the exclusive adjudication of disputes affecting important personal and property interests of both Indians and non-Indians." Federal review is allowed "only in habeas corpus proceedings."

17. *Trans-Canada Enterprises, Ltd. v. Muckleshoot Indian Tribe,* 634 F.2d 474 (9th Cir. 1980).

Facts: The Tribe enacted an ordinance prohibiting the conduct of business on the reservation without a tribal business license. Trans-Canada refused to comply with the tribal ordinance and began construction of a housing development within the boundaries of the reservation. The tribal court issued an injunction against further construction. After Trans-Canada filed suit in federal court, asserting violations of both the Constitution and the Indian Civil Rights Act, the district court enjoined enforcement of the tribal ordinance.

Issue: Did Trans-Canada have a cause of action in federal court?

Held: (1) There is no implied private right of action under the Indian Civil Rights Act, and "[t]he sole federal remedy for an alleged violation of the Act is application for federal habeas corpus relief."

(2) "Constitutional guarantees . . . are not applicable to the exercise of governmental powers by an Indian tribe except to the extent that they are made explicitly binding by the Constitution or are imposed by Congress."

18. *Escondido Mutual Water Co. v. La Jolla, Rincon, San Pasqual, Pauma, and Pala Bands of Mission Indians,* 466 U.S. 765 (1984).

Facts: Under the Federal Power Act (FPA), a hydroelectric project licensee sought to extend its license to divert water on or near Mission Indian reservations. The tribes opposed the license, and the Secretary of the Interior insisted that the licensing Commission prohibit the licensees from interfering with the tribes' use of a specified quantity of water.

Issues: What authority did the Secretary have over the licensing process? Could the tribes insist upon tribal consent to the operation of licensed facilities on reservation lands?

Held: (1) The FPA requires the Commission to accept, without modification, conditions the Secretary deems necessary for the adequate protection of federal reservations. This applies only to licenses for projects within the geographic boundaries of a reservation, not to licenses for projects which merely "affect" a reservation.

(2) Tribal consent to a project is not required. Tribal authority "to prevent a federal agency from carrying out its statutory responsibility . . . would seem to be inconsistent with [the tribe's] status." Moreover, the FPA was intended to be applied to reservation lands without tribal consent.

19. *United States v. White Mountain Apache Tribe,* 784 F.2d 917 (9th Cir. 1986).

Facts: The tribal court enjoined employees of the Department of the Interior from taking certain actions preparatory to United States participation in water rights litigation on behalf of the Tribe. The United States filed suit in federal district court, which enjoined the Tribe from interfering with United States action.

Issue: Does the Tribe's power to exclude non-members from the reservation extend to government employees?

Held: (1) "[T]he federal government, as trustee for the tribes, is under an affirmative obligation to assert water claims on its beneficiaries' behalf." Thus, "efforts by government agents or employees to prepare the claim are official duties."

(2) "The Tribe's effort to enjoin the work of any federal agent or employee in the performance of his official duties" is barred by the sovereign immunity of the United States.

(3) Tribal sovereignty cannot prevent "the federal government from exercising its superior sovereign powers," despite tribal charges of improper conduct of official business.

(4) "The district court had jurisdiction to determine the limits of the Tribe's power."

B. Statutory Relationship

General laws of Congress do not always apply to Indians, and the reason lies in the history of interactions between the United States and Indian tribes. As the federal government expanded its jurisdiction westward during the early eighteenth century, Indians generally were outside its control. They were separate governments which were to be dealt with in a manner similar to foreign states. In 1884, the Supreme Court clearly spelled out this relationship in *Elk v. Wilkins,* stating that Indians were not citizens of the United States, and that Congress' laws did not apply to them unless Congress clearly indicated their application. Even though citizenship was extended to all Indians in 1924, the attitude that Indians were somehow outside the reach of federal laws persisted.

The Supreme Court addressed that issue squarely in *Federal Power Commission v. Tuscarora* in 1960. Even though the discussion was not necessary to the holding, the Court made a point of stating "it is now well settled . . . that a general statute in terms applying to all persons includes Indians and their property interests." This holding was reaffirmed in the 1972 *Davis v. Morton* decision, when the Bureau of Indian Affairs asserted that the National Environmental Policy Act (NEPA) did not apply to federal actions on Indian lands. The Tenth Circuit found that NEPA, and other general statutes, applied to Indian circumstances unless Congress clearly stated otherwise.

One major exception exists to this basic rule. General laws do not apply to Indians if they conflict with specific rights granted Indians in treaties or statutes. One example of this exception with regard to a special statutory right came in 1974, when the Supreme Court in *Morton v. Mancari* held that preferential hiring of Indians by the Bureau of Indian Affairs did not violate the Equal Employment Opportunity Act or due process. The specific Indian right to a hiring preference, granted in an earlier statute, was not overcome by the later general act, since Congress had not manifested clear intent to nullify the preference.

In 1982, the Tenth Circuit in *Donovan v. Navajo Forest Products Industries* held that the Occupational Safety and Health Act, based on a system of workplace inspections for safety hazards, did not apply to a tribal enterprise on the Navajo Reservation because its application would abrogate the Navajo treaty right to exclude non-Indians, the OSHA inspectors, from the reservation.

In 1985, the Ninth Circuit explained and clarified the treaty-right exception to the *Tuscarora* rule in *Donovan v. Coeur d'Alene Tribal Farm.* The court emphasized that the right must be documented in a treaty, or must be one of a very narrowly construed number of rights inherent in tribal sovereignty and self-government. In this case, the court found that OSHA did not interfere with any of those narrow rights and, because the Coeur d'Alene Tribe had no treaty with the United States, the Tribe could not take advantage of the treaty right exception to *Tuscarora*. So, OSHA applied on the Coeur d'Alene Reservation.

In 1986, the Supreme Court found that treaty rights can be overcome by a general statute so long as that result is intended by Congress. The Court's *United States v. Dion* decision determined from circumstances surrounding the passage and amendment of the Eagle Protection Act that Congress intended to abrogate Indian treaty rights to hunt eagles on Indian reservations.

1. *Elk v. Wilkins,* 112 U.S. 94 (1884).

Facts: An Indian was denied the opportunity to register to vote, on the grounds that he was not a citizen of the United States. He claimed that he had severed his tribal relationships and had submitted totally to United States jurisdiction.

Issue: Is an Indian, born within the United States and voluntarily terminating his tribal relationship, a citizen of the United States?

Held: (1) Indians, who are not taxed, are not counted in determining congressional representation, and "[g]eneral acts of Congress did not apply to Indians, unless so expressed as to clearly manifest an intention to include them."

(2) Indians cannot become citizens on their own. This plaintiff "does not allege that the United States accepted his surrender [to its jurisdiction] or that he has ever been naturalized or taxed. . . . Nor is it contended . . . that there is any statute or treaty that makes him a citizen." Thus, he is not a citizen and has been deprived of no constitutional right.

2. *Federal Power Commission v. Tuscarora Indian Nation,* 362 U.S. 99 (1960).

Facts: The Federal Power Commission, acting under the Federal Power Act (FPA), licensed a project which required the taking of fee lands belonging to the Tuscarora Indian Nation, in return for just compensation.

Issue: Does the FPA authorize the taking of Tuscarora land?

Held: (1) The FPA restricts the taking of lands within a "reservation," which includes "tribal lands within Indian reservations . . . and other lands and interests in lands owned by the United States. . . ." Since "the lands involved are owned in fee simple by the Tuscarora Indian Nation and no 'interest' in them is 'owned by the United States,'. . . they are not within a 'reservation'."

(2) Even though the FPA is a general act of Congress, "it is now well settled . . . that a general statute in terms applying to all persons includes Indians and their property interests." Thus, the licensee has the authority to condemn the Tuscarora lands.

3. *Davis v. Morton,* 469 F.2d 593 (10th Cir. 1972).

Facts: Environmentalists complained that a 99-year lease granted by the Navajo Tribe, and approved by the U.S. government, to a subdivision developer did not meet the requirements of the National Environmental Policy Act (NEPA), 42 U.S.C. §§ 4321-4347, or the

Indian leasing statute, 25 U.S.C. § 415, which had an environmental provision.

Issue: Does NEPA apply to leases of Indian lands?

Held: (1) The United States' approval of leases of Indian lands constitutes "major federal action" within the meaning of NEPA. Under the rule in *Tuscarora,* this general federal statute applies to Indians in the absence of a clear congressional expression to the contrary.

(2) 25 U.S.C. § 415 only "reaffirms congressional intent" that environmental considerations apply to leases of Indian lands.

4. *Morton v. Mancari,* 417 U.S. 535 (1974).

Facts: Non-Indian Bureau of Indian Affairs employees challenged the Bureau's statutory policy of Indian preference in Bureau job promotion.

Issue: Did the Bureau policy of Indian preference violate either the 1972 Equal Employment Opportunity Act or the Due Process Clause of the Fifth Amendment of the Constitution?

Held: (1) Indian preference is not a racial preference. The preference is political in nature, intended to further Indian self-government and to make the Bureau more responsive to its constituent groups.

(2) Special treatment for Indian employees of the Bureau can be tied rationally to the fulfillment of Congress' obligations to Indians. Hence, due process is not violated.

(3) The specific statute (Indian preference) is not nullified by the general one (the 1972 Act) when there is no clear congressional intent to do so.

5. *Manygoates v. Kleppe,* 558 F.2d 556 (10th Cir. 1977).

Facts: Several Navajo tribal members sued to enjoin activities under a uranium exploration and mining agreement between the Navajo Tribe and Exxon Corporation. Plaintiffs argued that the Environmental Impact Statement (EIS), prepared by the Bureau of Indian Affairs and considered by the Secretary of the Interior in approving the agreement, was inadequate.

Issue: Was the Navajo Tribe an indispensable party to the action, whose nonjoinder because of sovereign immunity must result in dismissal of the suit? Was the Navajo Tribe adequately represented by the United States as guardian?

Held: (1) "[T]he duties and responsibilities of the Secretary [under the National Environmental Policy Act (NEPA)] may conflict with the interests of the Tribe. The Secretary must act in accord with the obligations imposed by NEPA. . . . When there is a conflict between the interest of the United States and the interest of Indians, representation of the Indians by the United States is not adequate."

(2) Although the Tribe is a necessary party to this action, "[a] holding that the EIS is inadequate does not necessarily result in prejudice to the Tribe. . . . Dismissal of the action for nonjoinder of the Tribe would produce an anomalous result. No one, except the Tribe, could seek review of an . . . [EIS] covering significant federal action . . . on Indian lands. NEPA is concerned with national environmental interests. Tribal interests may not coincide with national interests. We find nothing in NEPA which excepts Indian land from national environmental policy."

6. *Donovan v. Navajo Forest Products Industries*, 692 F.2d 709 (10th Cir. 1982).

Facts: Department of Labor personnel inspected the facilities of NFPI, an enterprise wholly owned and operated by the Navajo Tribe on the Navajo Reservation. NFPI was cited for numerous violations of the Occupational Safety and Health Act. NFPI contested the citation, claiming that the Secretary of Labor lacked jurisdiction.

Issue: Did the Occupational Safety and Health Act apply on the Navajo Reservation?

Held: (1) Under *Tuscarora*, general acts of Congress apply to Indians unless Congress exempts them. But, "[t]he *Tuscarora* rule does not apply to Indians if the application of the general statute would be in derogation of the Indians' treaty rights."

(2) The Navajo Treaty recognizes the right of the Navajo Tribe to exclude non-Indians from the Navajo Reservation, and the right to tribal self-government.

(3) "The Navajos have not voluntarily relinquished the power granted under Article II of the treaty. Neither has that power been divested by congressional enactment of OSHA. . . ." Thus, OSHA does not apply to NFPI.

7. *Donovan v. Coeur d'Alene Tribal Farm*, 751 F.2d 1113 (9th Cir. 1985).

Facts: A compliance officer from the Department of Labor conducted an inspection of the Coeur d'Alene Tribal Farm, a commercial enterprise wholly owned and operated by the Tribe on the reservation. The officer cited the Farm for violations of the Occupational Safety and Health Act. The Farm challenged the application of OSHA to its operations.

Issue: Did the Occupational Safety and Health Act apply on the Coeur d'Alene Reservation?

Held: (1) "A federal statute of general applicability that is silent on the issue of application to Indian tribes will not apply to them if: (1) the law touches 'exclusive rights of self-governance in purely intramural matters'; (2) the application of the law to the tribe would 'abrogate rights guaranteed by Indian treaties'; or (3) there is proof 'by legislative history or some other means that Congress intended [the law] not to apply to Indians on their reservation. . . .' "

(2) "In any of these three situations, Congress must *expressly* apply a statute to Indians before we will hold that it reaches them."

(3) The legislative history of OSHA and the surrounding circumstances of its passage indicate no congressional intent to exclude Indians from its coverage. Nor does OSHA interfere with tribal self-government over purely intramural matters such as tribal membership, inheritance, and domestic relations.

(4) "In this case . . . [unlike *NFPI*] there is no treaty between the Coeur d'Alene Tribe and the United States government. . . . Thus, the Farm cannot avail itself of the 'treaty rights' exception" and OSHA applies to the Farm.

8. *State of Washington, Department of Ecology v. United States Environmental Protection Agency*, 752 F.2d 1465 (9th Cir. 1985).

Facts: The State of Washington applied to the Environmental Protection Agency (EPA) for authority under the Resource Conservation and Recovery Act (RCRA) to administer the federal hazardous waste program within the state. EPA approved the application, but excluded Indian lands, over which EPA retained regulatory control of hazardous waste.

Issue: Does RCRA confer jurisdiction on the State to regulate all hazardous waste activities on Indian lands?

Held: (1) Neither the statute nor its legislative history discusses state regulation on Indian reservations. Thus, "[w]e must defer to the agency's interpretation" of the statute, "as long as the agency has adopted a reasonable construction of the statute."

(2) The statute must be interpreted "against the 'backdrop' of tribal sovereignty, especially when the statute affects an area in which the tribes historically have exercised their sovereign authority or contemporary policy encourages tribal self-government."

(3) RCRA does not "clearly evince . . . a Congressional purpose to revise federal Indian policy or to diminish the independence of Indian tribes."

(4) Under the EPA's interpretation of RCRA, it "can promote the ability of the tribes to govern themselves by allowing them to participate in hazardous waste management." Thus, the State does not have jurisdiction.

9. *Kerr-McGee Corp. v. Navajo Tribe of Indians,* 471 U.S. 195 (1985).
(*See* brief at III.C.12)

10. *United States v. Dion,* 476 U.S. 734 (1986).
(*See* brief at IV.C.14)

C. Individual Relationship

The special relationship between Indians and the United States government tends to be thought of in terms of governmental interactions. Although that aspect of the relationship is predominant, individual Indians also are affected. As early as 1916 in *United States v. Nice,* the Supreme Court held that despite the fact that an individual Indian was a citizen, his allotment was still held in trust by the federal government and he remained under the "national guardianship" of the United States. However, individual Indians most often have had to fight for some of the same rights as other citizens, despite their special status.

States frequently have attempted to exclude Indians from the benefits of citizenship on the basis of their separate political status. In the 1924 case *Piper v. Big Pine School District,* an Indian child was denied access to a state public school. The court ordered the school to admit her, confirming the right of Indian children to public education under the Equal Protection Clause of the Constitution. Similar cases have found constitutionally protected rights to access to state welfare benefits and voting in state elections.

Protections arising out of the federal-Indian relationship which are unique to individual Indians usually focus on traditional or unusual religious beliefs and practices. The First Amendment of the Constitution does not apply to Indian tribal governments and, as the court in *Native American Church v. Navajo Tribal Council* held, affords no protection against tribal regulation of religious practices. However, courts have uniformly held that Indian religions are protected against state and federal incursions by the First Amendment.

In 1964, the court in *People v. Woody* held that use of peyote, a narcotic regulated by state law, during an Indian religious ceremony was protected. An Indian prison inmate wearing long braided hair also has been protected by the Free Exercise Clause. However, in 1980 the *Badoni v. Higginson* court limited the exercise of Indian religious rights on non-Indian federal lands, finding instead that the federal government's interest in maintaining a storage reservoir's capacity outweighed the Indian religious interest. In 1988, the Supreme Court in *Lyng v. Northwest Indian Cemetery Protective Association* reached a similar conclusion. The Court found that, in the absence of government coercion or penalty, the proposed timber management and road construction activities would not violate the Free Exercise of Religion Clause of the First Amendment. The Supreme Court also specifically held that the American Indian Religious Freedom Act itself created no causes of action or individual rights. Most recently, the Court's decision in *Employment Division v. Smith* held that states could prohibit the religious use of peyote if the burden on religion was only an incidental effect of a neutral law of general application.

Individual Indians today are entitled to the same rights and privileges as are any other citizen. In addition, they are the beneficiaries of a federal guardianship. The principal disputes remaining over individual Indian rights seem to be those involving the application of the rights of American citizenship to unique Indian cultural traditions. Those battles likely will continue so long as there are distinct Indian cultures in this country.

1. *United States v. Nice,* 241 U.S. 591 (1916).

Facts: A non-Indian was prosecuted for selling whiskey to an Indian in violation of federal law. The Indian held an allotment under the General Allotment Act; the land was still in trust.

Issue: Did the allottees remain under "national guardianship" so that Congress could continue to regulate liquor sales to them despite the allotments and national citizenship?

Held: (1) "Citizenship is not incompatible with tribal existence or continued guardianship, and so may be conferred without . . . placing [the Indians] beyond the reach of Congressional regulations adopted for their protection."

(2) Only when the trust period expired did the General Allotment Act envision that the "national guardianship" would terminate; not upon the mere issuance of the allotments and trust patents.

2. *Piper v. Big Pine School District,* 193 Cal. 664, 226 P. 926 (1924).

Facts: An Indian child sought a court order compelling a state public school to admit her. The federal government maintained a school for Indians within the same school district, and the child was eligible to attend there.

Issue: Did the state school's refusal to admit the Indian pupil violate the Fourteenth Amendment's Equal Protection Clause?

Held: Even though increased attendance of Indian children will cause increased economic and administrative problems for the state's school district, the Constitution requires the school to admit pupils who are state residents and citizens, under the Equal Protection Clause.

3. *Acosta v. San Diego County,* 126 Cal. App. 2d 455, 272 P.2d 92 (1954).

Facts: A "needy Indian" was denied welfare benefits by the county on the basis that "reservation Indians are not residents of the county."

Issue: Does the Privileges and Immunities Clause of the Fourteenth Amendment entitle reservation Indians to state welfare benefits?

Held: (1) "Indians living on reservations . . . are citizens and residents of [the State] . . . they are endowed with the rights, privileges and immunities equal to those enjoyed by all other citizens and residents of the State," under the Fourteenth Amendment.

(2) Whether reservation Indians "are subject to state laws and taxation" is not pertinent. The State receives numerous economic benefits from the presence of the reservation within its borders.

4. *Allen v. Merrell,* 6 Utah 2d 32, 305 P.2d 490 (1956), *vacated and remanded,* 353 U.S. 932 (1957).

Facts: An Indian was denied the right to vote in a state government election pursuant to the State's definition of "resident," which excluded people living on reservations.

Issue: Did the denial violate the Fifteenth Amendment (denial of right to vote on account of race) or the Fourteenth Amendment (equal protection or privileges and immunities)?

Held: Because Indians receive substantial federal benefits, their real estate held in trust is not subject to state taxation, and they are not "conversant with activities of the outside world generally," they are not entitled to vote unless they take up residence free from the federal government and pay taxes.

Note: The state legislature later repealed the statute.

5. *Native American Church v. Navajo Tribal Council*, 272 F.2d 131 (10th Cir. 1959).

(*See* brief at II.A.10)

6. *People v. Woody*, 61 Cal. 2d 716, 40 Cal. Rptr. 69, 394 P.2d 813 (1964).

Facts: Indians were arrested under state narcotics laws for using peyote in a Native American Church ceremony.

Issue: Did the application of state law infringe on the Indians' First Amendment rights to free exercise of their religion, or did the State have a "compelling interest" in curtailing their religious freedom?

Held: (1) Peyote is "more than a sacrament." It is "itself an object of worship. . . . To forbid the use of peyote is to remove the theological heart of Peyotism."

(2) The State did not prove harmful consequences of peyote which outweighed the Indians' freedom of religion.

7. *Tooahnippah v. Hickel*, 397 U.S. 598 (1970).

Facts: The Regional Solicitor for the Department of the Interior disapproved an Indian's will, which disinherited an illegitimate daughter, on the grounds that the testamentary disposition was "inequitable."

Issue: Was the Regional Solicitor's action reviewable, and if so, under what standard of review?

Held: (1) Yes, the action is subject to judicial review.

(2) Although "it is not difficult to conceive of dispositions so lacking in rational basis that the Secretary's approval could reasonably be withheld," in this case the Regional Solicitor's action was "arbitrary and capricious."

(3) "The Indian's right to make inter vivos dispositions is limited and requires approval of the Secretary," but a public officer cannot "substitute his preference for that of an Indian testator" based upon subjective notions of "equity."

8. *Prince v. Board of Education*, 88 N.M. 548, 543 P.2d 1176 (1975).

Facts: Non-Indians challenged the Indians' right to vote in a school board and bond election on the grounds that the reservation lands, which were within the school district, were not subject to taxation.

Issue: Would restricting the vote to real estate owners and taxpayers violate constitutional guarantees of equal protection?

Held: (1) Ninety-seven percent of the District's taxes came from corporate lessees of Indian land.

(2) State laws restricting the vote to taxpayers and real estate owners would be a denial of equal protection.

9. *Teterud v. Burns,* 522 F.2d 357 (8th Cir. 1975).

Facts: An Indian inmate challenged a prison regulation prohibiting him from wearing long braided hair as, inter alia, violating his constitutional right to free exercise of religion.

Issue: Did the "interests of penal administration" outweigh the prisoner's rights to wear his hair long?

Held: (1) "The wearing of long braided hair [is] a tenet of the Indian religion sincerely held" by the prisoner. It need not be an "absolute tenet . . . practiced by all Indians."

(2) "The institutional needs of the penitentiary can be served by viable, less restrictive means. . . ."

10. *Badoni v. Higginson,* 638 F.2d 172 (10th Cir. 1980), *cert. denied,* 452 U.S. 954 (1981).

Facts: Certain Navajos had worshiped at Rainbow Bridge National Monument, off reservation, for over 100 years. The United States built a dam which created a lake under the Bridge. The National Park Service operated boats to take tourists to the Monument. As a result, the Indians could no longer worship there.

Issue: Did the United States have sufficient interest to interfere with the Indians' free exercise of religion?

Held: (1) "Analysis of a free exercise claim involves a two step process": Does the government action burden plaintiff's religion? If so, can the government establish an interest of "sufficient magnitude" to override the religious interest?

(2) The government's interest in maintaining the lake's storage capacity outweighs the religious interest.

(3) The National Park Service's existing regulations are sufficient to control tourist behavior. For the government to go further in regulating tourists to aid religious ceremonies would violate the constitutional restrictions regarding establishment of religions.

(4) No specific violations of the American Indian Religious Freedom Act were alleged.

11. *Lyng v. Northwest Indian Cemetery Protective Association,* 485 U.S. 439 (1988).

Facts: An association of Northwest Indians sued to enjoin the United States Forest Service from harvesting timber and constructing logging roads in a unit of a northern California National Forest. This unit is sacred to several Indian tribes, and specific sites are used for religious activities. The Indians alleged that the logging activities would violate the Free Exercise of Religion Clause of the United States Constitution.

Issue: Would the proposed activities infringe on the Indians' right to exercise their religion?

Held: (1) Although the Indians themselves are not unanimous in opposing the project, "we can assume that the threat to the efficacy of at least some religious practices is extremely grave."

(2) Accommodating these religious beliefs "could easily require de facto beneficial ownership [by the Indians] of some rather spacious tracts of public property. Even without anticipating future cases, the diminution of the Government's property rights, and the concomitant subsidy of the Indian religion, would in this case be far from trivial. . . ."

(3) In this case, there is no violation of the Free Exercise of Religion Clause because the affected individuals will not be coerced by governmental action into violating their religious beliefs, nor will the governmental action penalize religious activity. "The First Amendment must apply to all citizens alike, and it can give to none of them a veto over public programs that do not prohibit the free exercise of religion."

(4) In developing its plans for this project, the Forest Service has been extremely solicitous toward traditional Indian cultural and religious values. "Respondents, however, suggest that AIRFA [American Indian Religious Freedom Act] goes further and in effect enacts their interpretation of the First Amendment into statutory law. . . . This argument is without merit. . . . Nowhere in the law is there so much as a hint of any intent to create a cause of action or any judicially enforceable individual rights."

(5) The dissent suggests that this Court act as an arbiter in the conflict between the Indian and non-Indian cultures, and proposes a legal test whereby the Court would decide which public lands are indispensable to which religions, weighing the value of each governmentally threatened religious belief and practice. This approach "would require us to rule that some religious adherents misunderstand their own religious beliefs. We think such an approach cannot be squared with the Constitution or with our precedents, and that it would cast the judiciary in a role that we were never intend to play."

12. *Employment Division, Oregon Department of Human Resources v. Smith,* 58 U.S.L.W. 4433 (U.S. April 17, 1990).

Facts: Two members of the Native American Church were fired from their jobs for ingesting peyote during a ceremony and were later denied unemployment benefits. The use of peyote was prohibited by Oregon law.

Issue: Can Oregon prohibit the religious use of peyote? Was the denial of unemployment benefits constitutional?

Held: (1) The First Amendment allows governmental action burdening the exercise of religion so long as "prohibiting the exercise of religion . . . is not the object of the . . . [governmental action] but merely the incidental effect of a generally applicable and otherwise valid provision."

(2) The Court's decisions "have consistently held that the right of free exercise [of religion] does not relieve an individual of the obligation to comply with a 'valid and neutral law of general application on the ground that the law proscribes (or prescribes) conduct that his religion prescribes (or proscribes).' "

(3) Balancing the burden on religion against the compelling nature of the governmental interest is not called for in this case, since imposing the "compelling governmental interest" requirement would produce "a private right to ignore generally applicable laws--[which] is a constitutional anomaly."

(4) "Because respondents' ingestion of peyote was prohibited under Oregon law, and because that prohibition is constitutional, Oregon may, consistent with the Free Exercise Clause, deny respondents unemployment compensation when their dismissal results from use of the drug."

D. Trust Relationship

The most enduring characteristic of the interactions between Indian tribes and the United States government is the trust relationship. Chief Justice John Marshall in the 1831 *Cherokee Nation v. Georgia* decision first described the relationship between the government and the Indians as resembling "that of a ward to his guardian," and selected tenets of the common law of trusts have been applied to the relationship ever since. Government actions toward Indians, according to *Seminole Nation v. United States,* must adhere to "exacting fiduciary standards," and reflect good faith and fair dealing. Courts have found breaches of these general standards when the United States made inappropriate payments to a corrupt tribal council, invested Indian funds at less than the best market rates, and seized development opportunities legitimately belonging to a tribe.

Although most cases finding trust duties have involved the handling of money, government responsibilities are not that narrow. The Supreme Court in 1913 in *United States v. Sandoval* held that Congress determines the extent of the trust relationship, and affirmative governmental trust duties are found in federal statutes relating to Indians. The clearest example of this arose in *Joint Tribal Council of Passamaquoddy Tribe v. Morton.* In that case, even though the Passamaquoddy Tribe was not recognized by the United States, and therefore was not eligible for federal Indian services, the Indian Nonintercourse Act of 1790 established a trust relationship between the Tribe and the federal government. The Act required the government to protect the title to Indian lands, including Passamaquoddy aboriginal land, as a trust duty.

More recently, federal courts have examined the trust relationship in detail, particularly regarding claims for money damages made by tribes against the United States for alleged breaches of trust duties. In 1983, the Supreme Court in *United States v. Mitchell (II)* held that statutes and regulations mandating the pervasive involvement of the Secretary of the Interior in management of Indian timber give rise to fiduciary obligations on the part of the government. Breach of these obligations may give rise to money damages against the United States. The Court of Claims in the 1986 case *Navajo Tribe v. United States* awarded damages to the Tribe for the government's failure to follow statutory and regulatory standards in managing tribal timber resources. However, the court refused to find a breach of fiduciary duty regarding overgrazing in the forest, despite the failure of the government to follow congressional mandates. In that case, the Tribe supported the grazing practices, and Indian cultural traditions were involved.

Although courts normally judge the government's actions according to the common law standards binding a trustee, there are exceptions. As sometimes happens, in *Nevada v. United States* the Secretary of the Interior was obliged by Congress to represent Indian interests as trustee and to carry out potentially conflicting statutory obligations. The Supreme Court held that in such cases, the Secretary cannot be judged by "the fastidious standards of a private fiduciary," and can represent both interests.

The federal trust relationship with Indians has served as a backdrop for government actions toward Indians and their property. However, tribes more and more are challenging those actions when they run counter to tribal expectations. Breach of trust cases are increasing, particularly in the area of natural resource management, and the federal government will be held to clear, statutory trust standards. However, the court's decision in *Navajo Tribe v. United States* indicates that tribal support for or acquiescence in actions violating those standards may subvert tribal efforts to enforce strict trust duties.

1. *Cherokee Nation v. Georgia,* 30 U.S. (5 Pet.) 1 (1831)

   (*See* brief at II.A.3)

2. *United States v. Sandoval,* 231 U.S. 28 (1913)

   (*See* brief at II.A.8)

3. *Seminole Nation v. United States,* 316 U.S. 286 (1942).

Facts: An 1856 treaty required payments from the United States to tribal members to be distributed per capita. The United States paid part of the money instead to the tribal council, which was defrauding tribal members, and directly to creditors.

Issue: Was the United States liable, as trustee, for misdirecting these payments?

Held: (1) "In carrying out its treaty obligations with the Indian tribes, the Government is something more than a mere contracting party. . . . Its conduct . . . should be judged by the most exacting fiduciary standards."

(2) If the United States knew that the tribal council was defrauding its members, the payments to the council were "a clear breach of the Government's fiduciary obligation."

4. *Navajo Tribe of Indians v. United States,* 364 F.2d 320 (Ct. Cl. 1966).

Facts: An oil company leased Navajo land for drilling. The oil company discovered helium, and transferred the lease to the Bureau of Mines without the Tribe's knowledge.

Issue: Was the United States liable as fiduciary?

Held: (1) The United States is judged by " 'the most exacting fiduciary standards.' "

(2) The United States had a conflict of interest within the Department of the Interior.

(3) A fiduciary may not learn of an opportunity, prevent the beneficiary from getting it, and seize it for himself.

5. *Manchester Band of Pomo Indians v. United States,* 363 F. Supp. 1238 (N.D. Cal. 1973).

Facts: The Bureau of Indian Affairs did not invest the Band's money in the best depositories. It invested some of the money in the United States Treasury at low interest, and received no interest at all for some of the money.

Issue: Was the United States liable in damages for breach of its duty as trustee toward the Indians?

Held: (1) The Government's conduct is "measured by the same standards applicable to private trustees."

(2) The Bureau of Indian Affairs is liable for this breach of fiduciary duty.

6. *Pyramid Lake Paiute Tribe of Indians v. Morton,* 354 F. Supp. 252 (D.D.C. 1973).

Facts: The Secretary of the Interior promulgated regulations governing the diversion of water from a river flowing into Pyramid Lake within the Pyramid Lake Paiute Indian Reservation. The Tribe depends on the lake for its livelihood. Within these regulations, in determining the amount to be diverted away from the river to the Truckee-Carson Irrigation District, the Secretary based his decision on a "judgment call." The Tribe challenged the regulations.

Issue: Were the Secretary's regulations valid?

Held: "A 'judgment call' was simply not legally permissible. The Secretary's duty was not to determine a basis for allocating water" that satisfied all of the parties. To carry out his fiduciary duty, the Secretary "was obliged to formulate a closely developed regulation that would preserve water for the Tribe."

7. *Joint Tribal Council of Passamaquoddy Tribe v. Morton,* 528 F.2d 370 (1st Cir. 1975).

Facts: The Tribe sought a declaratory judgment that it was entitled to federal protection under the Indian Nonintercourse Act of 1790, in the form of legal assistance in an action against the State of Maine for the wrongful taking of the Tribe's aboriginal lands.

Issue: Was there a trust relationship between the United States and the Tribe, giving rise to a duty to protect the Tribe and its property?

Held: (1) The Nonintercourse Act established a trust relationship, even though the Passamaquoddy Tribe had not been recognized.

(2) Under the Nonintercourse Act, the federal government was obliged to protect the lands of "any tribe of Indians."

(3) "[T]he federal government may not decline to litigate on the sole ground that there is no trust relationship."

8. *United States v. Sioux Nation of Indians,* 448 U.S. 371 (1980).

Facts: In 1877, Congress enacted into law an "agreement" ceding the Black Hills to the federal government. The agreement was signed by only 10 percent of the adult males of the Tribe, despite an 1868 Treaty which required that no further cessions could be made without the approval of 75 percent of the adult males.

Issue: Was the 1877 Act a "taking," compensable under the Fifth Amendment, or merely the management of tribal property to promote the Tribe's welfare?

Held: (1) Although "tribal lands are subject to Congress' power to control and manage the tribe's affairs," this power "is subject to limitations inhering in a guardianship and to pertinent constitutional restrictions."

(2) Although the traditional view of the management of Indian affairs is that it is a political matter not reviewable by the courts, later cases indicate that "takings" of Indian property are reviewable.

(3) The appropriate test of this action is "whether Congress has made a good faith effort to give the Indians the full value of their lands."

(4) The United States is obliged to compensate the Sioux Tribe for taking the Black Hills, for as trustee, the government did not "give the ward the fair equivalent" of what was acquired.

9. *United States v. Mitchell (I),* 445 U.S. 535 (1980).

Facts: Allottees on the Quinault Reservation sought damages from the United States for mismanagement of timber resources.

Issue: Does the General Allotment Act of 1887 create a fiduciary duty on the part of the United States to manage timber properly, and does it constitute a waiver of sovereign immunity?

Held: (1) The General Allotment Act "created only a limited trust relationship between the United States and the allottee that does not impose any duty upon the Government to manage timber resources."

(2) Since there is no general trust duty under the General Allotment Act to manage timber, the Court did not have to decide whether the United States had waived its sovereign immunity.

(3) Other statutes or treaties creating trust duties may give rise to money damages against the United States for mismanagement of timber resources.

10. *United States v. Mitchell (II)*, 463 U.S. 206 (1983).

Facts: Holders of allotments sued the federal government for mismanagement of timber resources on trust lands.

Issue: Do any other statutes render the United States liable for damages resulting from timber mismanagement on Indian trust lands?

Held: (1) The Tucker Act of 1887 constitutes a waiver of United States sovereign immunity in the Court of Claims for claims to money damages.

(2) The Secretary of the Interior's "pervasive role" in Indian timber management, as established by several statutes and regulations, evidences a fiduciary relationship, the breach of which gives rise to money damages against the United States.

11. *Nevada v. United States*, 463 U.S. 110 (1983).

(*See* brief at IV.D.7)

12. *Navajo Tribe of Indians v. United States*, 9 Ct. Cl. 336 (1986).

Facts: The Navajo Tribe sued to recover damages for the alleged breach of fiduciary duties by the United States, regarding the management of the tribal forest from 1880 to the present.

Issue: Was the United States liable for damages?

Held: (1) Government's failure to collect damages for the Tribe from a lumber company for breach of the lumber company's contract was a breach of the government's fiduciary obligation to the Tribe.

(2) Government did not have to cut the maximum amount of timber every year, when Indian funds to finance such harvest were not available and when time was required to train Indians in logging. However, the government abused its discretion by failing to pursue a smaller reasonable harvest each year.

(3) Where the government had a treaty obligation to construct reservation facilities, it was not liable to the Tribe for stumpage charges for lumber used to construct the facilities.

(4) As trustee, the government was not liable to pay for tribal lumber used to improve the trust res.

(5) If the government historically was responsible for building and maintaining Indian agencies, it must pay the Tribe stumpage charges for lumber used for those purposes.

(6) By failing to ensure that logging methods met regulatory standards, the government breached its trust obligations to the Tribe.

(7) Government did not violate its fiduciary duty by not stopping overgrazing in the tribal forest, where the Tribe supported the grazing practices and where cultural and traditional factors were involved.

III. JURISDICTION

Three governmental entities compete for jurisdiction over civil and criminal matters involving Indians: Indian tribal governments, state governments, and the federal government. Two factors are most important in determining appropriate jurisdiction. First, are any of the involved parties Indians? An Indian has generally been defined as a person with Indian blood who is a member of a federally recognized tribe. There is an underlying limited presumption that Indian tribal governments have personal jurisdiction over their own tribal members.

The second consideration involves whether the subject event occurred within or outside of "Indian country." Congress defined "Indian country," in 18 U.S.C. § 1151, as including all land within the limits of an Indian reservation under federal jurisdiction, all "dependent Indian communities," and all Indian allotments still held in trust by the United States. Under this definition, land owned by non-Indians can be Indian country if it is within an Indian reservation. Further, rights-of-way running through Indian reservations or allotments are Indian country. In 1975, the United States Supreme Court in *De Coteau v. District County Court* held that the concept of Indian country applies to all jurisdictional matters, civil and criminal. Another underlying limited presumption is that Indian tribal governments have subject matter jurisdiction over activities taking place in Indian country.

Despite presumptions of tribal jurisdiction, the federal government has taken broad jurisdiction over crimes by Indians in Indian country. Beginning with the Major Crimes Act of 1885, Congress has strictly limited tribal criminal jurisdiction. Although states historically have been excluded from any jurisdiction over Indian country, that general exclusion has been subject to substantial statutory and judicial exception. In 1953, Congress passed the most important of these exceptions, Public Law 280, which granted broad civil and criminal jurisdiction over Indian country to five named states. Although other states were permitted to assume jurisdiction under Public Law 280, and several have done so, the Indian Civil Rights Act of 1968 provided that thereafter no state could assume jurisdiction without tribal consent.

Although federal legislation, and federal courts, have made substantial inroads into the jurisdictional reach of traditional tribal sovereignty, that sovereignty continues to exist. Tribal powers are inherent, not derived from the federal government. As sovereigns, tribes exercise jurisdiction over their own affairs unless some federal exercise of power has altered tribal sovereignty. In fact, some recent federal legislation, such as the Indian Child Welfare Act of 1978, supports tribal sovereignty in areas vital to tribal interests. Court decisions addressing the issue of jurisdiction in Indian country reflect the struggles among federal, state, and tribal governments to find their appropriate roles.

A. Civil Jurisdiction

In civil matters, the federal government has not superseded tribal and state jurisdiction to the extent that it has in the criminal area. Consequently, civil contests involving Indians and Indian country most often find Indian tribes and states each trying to assert their jurisdictional power. State jurisdiction under Public Law 280 must be considered, but its application is limited. Without Public Law 280 jurisdiction, the courts usually make jurisdictional determinations based on the inherent interest of each sovereign in the matter at issue.

Jurisdiction in cases involving personal interests frequently depends on where events took place and who the parties are. State courts generally have jurisdiction over civil suits against Indian defendants which arise outside Indian country, and over actions by non-Indians against non-Indians which arise in Indian country. But, tribal governments retain extensive jurisdiction over civil matters involving tribal members or affecting tribal interests.

Courts increasingly have acknowledged tribal governmental interest and jurisdiction in regulatory matters. Issues dealing with the administration of land areas and populations within the boundaries of Indian reservations more and more are considered the realm of tribal governments. Disputes over personal relationships between tribal members and tribal cultural integrity have consistently been held to be within tribal governmental jurisdiction.

Cases with these jurisdictional concerns frequently become questions of which government has the largest stake in the outcome. As tribes have become more competent and assertive in their governmental capabilities, courts have drawn finer and finer lines between their interests and those of the states. This struggle for jurisdiction shows no signs of abating.

1. General Civil Jurisdiction

As early as 1832, in *Worcester v. Georgia* the Supreme Court held that Indian nations retained the inherent sovereign power of self-government, and state laws did not apply to Indian country. Courts have continued to recognize this idea of tribal sovereignty, even to the point of recognizing tribal immunity from suit, as held in *Morgan v. Colorado River Indian Tribe.* However, since *Worcester,* states have increasingly inserted themselves into jurisdictional contests with Indians.

During the termination era in 1953, Congress passed Public Law 280, conferring general civil jurisdiction, as well as criminal, over Indians and Indian lands in certain states, with options for other states to take over such jurisdiction at their discretion. In the absence of Public Law 280, however, tribes retain exclusive jurisdiction over civil suits against a tribal member for claims arising in Indian country. When one of the parties is not an Indian, or if the action arises outside of Indian country, state jurisdictional incursions have become more frequent.

The most important recognition of potential state authority came in 1958 in *Williams v. Lee.* The Supreme Court acknowledged that states could exercise jurisdiction over cases arising in Indian country, but not if the state action infringed on a tribe's right to self-government. Later cases have found state jurisdiction over reservation Indians if the dispute arises off-reservation, as long as the state action did not harm tribal self-government. This jurisdiction is sufficient to allow service of process by the state on the reservation.

Recently, Indian tribes have more successfully controlled jurisdictional issues. Despite limits on state jurisdiction, the court in *Three Affiliated Tribes v. Wold Engineering* held that tribes and tribal members can use state courts to pursue non-Indians over Indian country claims. *Babbit Ford v. Navajo Indian Tribe* determined that non-Indians doing business on the reservation voluntarily enter tribal jurisdiction and are bound by it. In *Santa Clara Pueblo v.*

Martinez, arising under the federal Indian Civil Rights Act, the Supreme Court held that the tribal court was the only possible forum, and even federal review was restricted to habeas corpus actions.

A recent Supreme Court decision on tribal jurisdiction, *National Farmers Union Insurance Company v. Crow Tribe* in 1985, both cements the authority of Indian tribes in Indian country and imposes federal safeguards. The case arose on non-Indian land within a reservation and involved an injury to a tribal member. When the non-Indian defendant went to federal court to challenge tribal jurisdiction, the Supreme Court stated that the appropriate body to determine the extent of tribal jurisdiction was the tribal court itself. However, the federal courts were available, upon exhaustion of tribal appeals, to determine whether the tribal court had exceeded its jurisdiction. This may limit tribal/state jurisdictional disputes, since general civil jurisdiction in Indian country apparently will be determined by the involved tribal court, subject only to narrow federal review.

The *National Farmers Union* holding has been followed and strengthened in the recent 1987 case, *Iowa Mutual Insurance Company v. LaPlante.* The Supreme Court held that a federal court may not exercise diversity jurisdiction over a dispute also pending before a tribal court until the tribal court has had the chance to determine its own jurisdiction. In addition, the alleged incompetence and local bias of tribal courts cannot overcome the federal policy of deference to tribal courts.

1. *Worcester v. Georgia,* 31 U.S. (6 Pet.) 515 (1832).

   (*See* brief at II.A.4)

2. *Williams v. Lee,* 358 U.S. 217 (1959).

Facts: A federally licensed non-Indian trader sued a Navajo tribal member in state court for a debt arising on the reservation.

Issue: Did the state court have jurisdiction?

Held: (1) The *Worcester* rule that state laws do not apply to Indians on their reservations has since been modified "where essential tribal relations were not involved and where the rights of Indians would not be jeopardized." But, if "state action infringed on the right of reservation Indians to make their own laws and be ruled by them," such action was invalid.

(2) If the Tribe's authority over reservation transactions is to be taken away, "it is for Congress to do it."

3. *Paiz v. Hughes,* 76 N.M. 562, 417 P.2d 51 (1966).

Facts: An Indian sued a non-Indian in state court over an automobile accident on the Jicarilla Apache Reservation.

Issue: Did the state court have subject matter jurisdiction over the tort?

Held: (1) "An Indian has the same rights as are accorded to any other person to invoke the jurisdiction of State courts to protect his legal rights in matters not affecting either the Federal Government or tribal relations."

(2) Permitting this action for personal injuries and wrongful death will not affect the Tribe's rights "to make their own laws and be ruled by them," nor will it affect the rights of the Federal Government.

4. *Morgan v. Colorado River Indian Tribe,* 103 Ariz. 425, 443 P.2d 421 (1968).

Facts: A wrongful death action was brought against the Tribe based on a boating accident on a tribally operated Marina Park. The accident took place off-reservation.

Issue: Could state courts take jurisdiction?

Held: (1) The Tribe is immune from suit. It cannot be sued "without its consent or the consent of Congress."

(2) The fact that the Tribe was incorporated under the Indian Reorganization Act of 1934 and engaged in a commercial enterprise was immaterial.

5. *Kennerly v. District Court of Montana,* 400 U.S. 423 (1971).

Facts: Indians were sued in state court on a debt for food bought from a grocery store on the reservation. The Tribe had passed a resolution stating that the tribal court and the State would have concurrent jurisdiction of suits against tribal members.

Issue: Was the tribal resolution valid to confer state jurisdiction?

Held: (1) Public Law 280 is the method for states to assume jurisdiction over reservations. Here, the State had not done so. The Tribe cannot unilaterally confer jurisdiction on the State.

(2) The tribal "consent" was not a valid consent under the 1968 amendments to P.L. 280. Consent must be manifested by a majority vote of the Tribe, not by a tribal council resolution.

6. *State Securities v. Anderson,* 84 N.M. 629, 506 P.2d 786 (1973).

Facts: An Indian was served with process on the reservation pursuant to a state court order. The state action was based on a contract made off-reservation.

Issue: Did the state court have personal jurisdiction to justify on-reservation service of process?

Held: (1) The State has concurrent personal jurisdiction, with the tribal court, over an Indian on the reservation, arising from an off-reservation contract.

(2) Such concurrent personal jurisdiction does not interfere with tribal self-government.

(3) To hold that the tribal court had exclusive jurisdiction would result in "shielding Indians from obligations incurred off the reservation."

7. *Schantz v. White Lightning,* 231 N.W.2d 812 (N.D. 1975).

Facts: A non-Indian passenger and driver of one car brought an action in state court against the Indian driver of the second car, arising out of an accident on the Standing Rock Reservation. The federal court had already ruled that it had no federal question jurisdiction. The tribal court's jurisdiction over non-Indian defendants was limited to $300. The plaintiffs sought to recover from the State's "Unsatisfied Judgment Fund."

Issue: Did the state court have subject matter jurisdiction over the tort?

Held: (1) Highways within a reservation are a part of Indian country.

(2) The court refuses to authorize piecemeal jurisdiction over reservation highways.

(3) The Unsatisfied Judgment Fund is not a party defendant so as to allow jurisdiction over a "non-Indian."

8. *Brough v. Appawora,* 553 P.2d 934 (Utah 1976), *vacated and remanded,* 431 U.S. 901 (1977).

Facts: A non-Indian sought to recover in state court against an Indian for injuries suffered in country that may have been part of the Ute Reservation.

Issue: Did the state court have subject matter jurisdiction over the tort?

Held: (1) The Ute Nation "no longer exists," so their treaty is no longer of any force or effect.

(2) The land on which the accident occurred was a disestablished part of the former reservation, thus "no longer Indian Country."

(3) It "would be in contravention of the due process clause" to allow an Indian to be immune from tort accountability simply because of the venue of the tort.

Note: Enforcement was subsequently enjoined by a federal court, which addressed the diminishment issue in greater detail.

9. *Little Horn State Bank v. Stops*, 555 P.2d 211 (Mont. 1976), *cert. denied*, 431 U.S. 924 (1977).

Facts: An Indian borrowed money off the reservation and failed to pay it back. Process was served on the reservation, and the state court ordered the sheriff to garnish the debtor's wages earned on the reservation.

Issue: May a state court order the levying or executing against Indian property on the reservation in satisfaction of a state court judgment relating to an off-reservation transaction?

Held: (1) The court had both subject matter and personal jurisdiction.

(2) The court, having jurisdiction to render a judgment, also has power to enforce the judgment through a writ of execution.

(3) The case is distinct from *Williams v. Lee* in that the underlying transaction arose off the reservation. Moreover, the tribal court would not have exercised jurisdiction in this case.

10. *Santa Clara Pueblo v. Martinez*, 436 U.S. 49 (1978).

(*See* brief at II.A.16)

11. *Washington v. Confederated Bands and Tribes of the Yakima Indian Reservation*, 439 U.S. 463 (1979).

Facts: The State assumed Public Law 280 jurisdiction only over fee lands, and over tribal trust or allotted lands where non-Indians were involved. The state law excepted from state jurisdiction Indians on trust or allotted lands, except for eight categories (domestic relations, school attendance, adoptions, motor vehicles, etc.). Also, the State assumed jurisdiction by legislation, rather than by amending the state constitution, which contained a disclaimer of authority over Indian country.

Issue: Was the assumption of jurisdiction valid without constitutional amendment? Could the State "pick and choose" partial jurisdiction over the reservation?

Held: (1) P.L. 280 did not require states with disclaimers to amend their constitutions before assuming jurisdiction. State legislation was sufficient.

(2) The State could assume less-than-full P.L. 280 jurisdiction.

(3) Although state legislation may not normally single out Indians in legislation, it may do so here, where federal law enables the State to act, without violating the Fourteenth Amendment's Equal Protection Clause.

12. *Joe v. Marcum,* 621 F.2d 358 (10th Cir. 1980).

Facts: An Indian borrowed money off the reservation and failed to pay it back. State court service was made on the reservation, and a default judgment was entered. A writ of garnishment was then issued against the debtor's on-reservation employer, a non-Indian company. The Navajo Tribal Code did not allow for garnishment, but did permit execution on specific property.

Issue: Did the state court have jurisdiction to order garnishment, in satisfaction of the default judgment?

Held: (1) Garnishment runs counter to Navajo policy, and impinges on tribal sovereignty.

(2) "The garnishment residence is located on the reservation and represents wages due for services rendered by [the Indian debtor to his non-Indian employer] on the reservation." Thus, garnishment was not permissible as "ancillary" to the default judgment.

13. *Three Affiliated Tribes v. Wold Engineering,* 321 N.W.2d 510 (N.D. 1982), *vacated,* 467 U.S. 138 (1984), *on remand,* 364 N.W.2d 98 (N.D. 1985).

Facts: The Tribe sued a non-Indian company in state court for breach of a contract which arose within the reservation. The State's enabling act disclaimed jurisdiction over Indian lands, and the State's jurisdictional statute pursuant to Public Law 280 required Indian acceptance of state jurisdiction. The tribal code did not permit claims against non-Indians without agreement of the parties.

Issue: Did the state court have jurisdiction? Had jurisdiction been disclaimed?

Held: (1) "Tribal self-government is not impeded when a State allows an Indian to enter its courts on equal terms with other persons to seek relief against a non-Indian concerning a claim arising in Indian Country."

(2) P.L. 280 did not divest states of preexisting jurisdiction, nor did it authorize states to disclaim preexisting jurisdiction.

(3) The enabling act's disclaimer did not prohibit Indians "from entering state courts to pursue judicial remedies against non-Indians."

(4) Although the Supreme Court does not have "authority to revise the North Dakota Supreme Court's interpretation of state jurisdictional law," in this case the state supreme court's interpretation was likely to have been based on "a misconception of federal law" (P.L. 280). The case is remanded to state court for reconsideration in light of federal law as explained, and the equal protection question is not reached.

14. *Babbit Ford, Inc. v. Navajo Indian Tribe,* 710 F.2d 587 (9th Cir. 1983), *cert. denied,* 466 U.S. 926 (1984).

Facts: Non-Indian car dealers entered the Navajo Reservation and repossessed automobiles purchased by tribal members now in default of their purchase contracts. Sales and delivery took place off-reservation. Repossessions violated the Navajo Tribal Code, and the tribal court imposed civil damages against the car dealers.

Issue: Did the tribal court have jurisdiction?

Held: (1) "The power to exercise tribal civil authority over non-Indians derives not only from the tribe's inherent powers necessary to self-government and territorial management, but also from the power to exclude nonmembers from tribal land."

(2) Tribal regulations over property repossession are designed to keep the peace and protect the health and safety of tribal members. Thus, they are an appropriate exercise of tribal self-government.

(3) The car dealers "conducted business with tribal members, and they must enter tribal lands to repossess the . . . automobiles. By doing so, they have entered the Tribe's jurisdiction."

(4) The Tribe's failure to adopt a constitution under the Indian Reorganization Act (IRA) does not divest the Tribe of jurisdiction, since the IRA did not require "a tribe to adopt a constitution before exercising civil jurisdiction over non-Indians."

15. *National Farmers Union Insurance Co. v. Crow Tribe of Indians,* 471 U.S. 845 (1985).

Facts: An Indian child was injured in an accident on the grounds of a school on state land within the reservation. The child's guardian sued the school district in tribal court, and a default judgment was entered against the school district. The school district filed suit against the Tribe in federal court for a permanent injunction against execution of the tribal court judgment.

Issue: Did the tribal court have jurisdiction? Is the jurisdictional issue a federal question, reviewable by the federal courts?

Held: (1) "[W]hether an Indian tribe retains the power to compel a non-Indian property owner to submit to the civil jurisdiction of a tribal court is . . . [a question] that must be answered by reference to federal law. . . ." Thus, "a federal court may determine under . . . [28 U.S.C. § 1331] whether a tribal court has exceeded the lawful limits of its jurisdiction."

(2) Determination of the extent of tribal jurisdiction requires an examination of tribal sovereignty and associated federal statutes, policies, and judicial decisions. "We believe that examination should be conducted in the first instance in the Tribal Court itself." Consequently, "[u]ntil petitioners have exhausted the remedies available to them in the Tribal Court system . . . it would be premature for a federal court to consider any relief."

16. *Iowa Mutual Insurance Co. v. LaPlante,* 480 U.S. 9 (1987).

Facts: A Blackfeet Indian tribal member was injured in an accident while driving a cattle truck on the reservation. When the involved insurance company denied coverage, the tribal member filed suit in Blackfeet Tribal Court against the insurance company alleging a bad-faith refusal to settle. The insurance company moved to dismiss the complaint for lack of jurisdiction, but the tribal court concluded that it had subject matter jurisdiction. Before the Tribal Court of Appeals had an opportunity for appellate review, the insurance company filed suit in federal district court, alleging diversity jurisdiction. The district court dismissed the complaint for lack of subject matter jurisdiction.

Issue: Did the tribal court have jurisdiction? Does the federal diversity statute override the federal policy of deference to tribal courts?

Held: (1) The exhaustion rule of *National Farmers Union* requires that, regardless of the basis for jurisdiction, federal courts should stay proceedings to allow the tribal court the opportunity to determine its own jurisdiction, in order to avoid competing with the tribal courts and infringing on their judicial authority. Alleged local bias and incompetence of the tribal courts cannot overcome this deference.

(2) "At a minimum, exhaustion of tribal remedies means that tribal appellate courts must have the opportunity to review the determinations of the lower tribal courts."

(3) There is no "indication that Congress intended the diversity statute to limit the jurisdiction of the tribal courts, [and] we decline . . . to hold that tribal sovereignty can be impaired in this fashion."

(4) The tribal court's determination of jurisdiction in this case ultimately is subject to review in federal court. "Unless a federal

court determines that the Tribal Court lacked jurisdiction, however, proper deference to the tribal court system precludes relitigation of issues raised by the LaPlante's bad-faith claim and resolved in the Tribal Courts."

2. Regulatory Jurisdiction

State and Indian tribal jurisdictional disputes are most evident in the regulation of property and personal activities. Although these disputes generally have arisen only in the recent past, after Indian tribal governments became more capable of regulation, they reflect trends similar to other jurisdictional contests. One area of conflict, off-reservation treaty rights, generally has been resolved, as reflected in *Puyallup Tribe v. Department of Game.* The Supreme Court found that state regulation of Indian treaty fishing rights was limited to non-discriminatory, reasonable, and necessary measures for the conservation of the fishery.

Tribal regulatory power was recognized in 1974 in *Wauneka v. Campbell* as part of an inherent sovereign police power. Against that background, state regulation on the reservation would infringe on tribal self-government. One year later, the Supreme Court in *United States v. Mazurie* confirmed a congressional delegation of authority to tribes, made possible because of tribal attributes of sovereignty. Despite this trend, *Norvell v. Sangre de Cristo Development* held that where states can show appropriate interests, state land use regulations that did not interfere with tribal government were enforceable.

Later courts found distinctions between state laws that were prohibitory in nature and those that were regulatory. *United States v. Marcyes* found state fireworks laws applicable on an Indian reservation because they were prohibitory, involving the health and welfare of all citizens and, therefore, incorporated into the Assimilative Crimes Act. The *Seminole Tribe v. Butterworth* court, on the other hand, found state bingo laws regulatory in nature and not applicable to Indian tribes. The Supreme Court in *California v. Cabazon Band of Mission Indians* in 1987 made a similar ruling regarding state and county regulation of an Indian bingo enterprise.

In 1981, the Supreme Court summarized the general rule for determining regulatory jurisdiction in Indian country, even on non-Indian lands, in *Montana v. United States.* Tribal jurisdiction is paramount where the activity in question threatens the tribe's economic or political security, or the health and welfare of tribal members. This clear statement was confused somewhat in 1983 when the Court in *Rice v. Rehner* held state liquor laws paramount because there was no tradition of tribal self-government over the liquor trade.

Despite somewhat confusing and overlapping tests for determining whether tribal or state regulation predominates in Indian country, federal control potentially is supreme. In 1986, the court in *United States v. Eberhardt* held that the Secretary of the Interior has authority from Congress to regulate Indian property in the best interests of the Indian people. This power was confirmed again in 1987, when the court in *Northern Arapahoe Tribe v. Hodel* upheld the Secretary's imposition of a game code regulating hunting and fishing on the reservation. Although this power exists, it is exercised today only under limited circumstances, assuring continued disputes between tribes and states.

The most recent case involving civil regulatory jurisdiction in Indian country graphically displays the complex and often-confused nature of the problem. The Supreme Court in *Brendale v. Confederated Bands and Tribes of the Yakima Indian Nation* in 1989 issued three separate opinions, each dealing with three consolidated cases, which resulted in a cumbersome compromise result. Despite the extreme split in opinions among the justices, they all relied at least in part on the concept of relative governmental interest as determinative of civil jurisdiction in Indian country.

1. *Puyallup Tribe v. Department of Game (Puyallup I),* 391 U.S. 392 (1968).

(*See* brief at IV.C.5)

2. *Wauneka v. Campbell,* 22 Ariz. App. 287, 526 P.2d 1085 (1974).

Facts: The Navajo Tribal Code required tribal members to have state driver's licenses.

Issue: Did the State's "Safety Responsibility Act," governing revocation of state licenses and contained in a different chapter of the state statutes, apply to tribal members?

Held: (1) The Navajo Tribe has its own police power. Thus, the State's license revocation law infringes on tribal self-government, particularly as that law carries criminal sanctions and involves judicial review.

(2) The State's licensing law and the revocation law have two

distinct purposes: safety and the collection of damages. The Tribe's adoption of one does not imply adoption of the other.

(3) The State had not adopted jurisdiction under P.L. 280.

3. *Norvell v. Sangre de Cristo Development Co.*, 372 F. Supp. 348 (D.N.M. 1974), *reversed on jurisdictional grounds*, 519 F.2d 370 (10th Cir. 1975).

Facts: The Tribe leased land to a non-Indian development company for development of a subdivision for non-Indians near Santa Fe. The lease was approved by the Secretary of the Interior, who had promulgated a regulation, pursuant to a federal statute delegating lease approval to the Secretary, proscribing the operation of state land use laws on leased Indian property.

Issue: Were the State's land subdivision act and construction licensing act preempted by federal law? Did they infringe on tribal self-government?

Held: (1) The Secretary's regulation was invalid, because it did not implement a specific act of Congress. The act relied on by the Secretary did not, at the time of the lease, vest the Secretary with "authority to regulate such things as construction, water, and land subdivision."

(2) The State's laws did not interfere with tribal self-government. The statutes were designed to protect state citizens against fraudulent subdivision schemes and substandard construction, and "only remotely, if at all," affect the Tribe.

4. *United States v. Mazurie*, 419 U.S. 544 (1975).

Facts: Non-Indians were convicted under federal law for introducing liquor into Indian country, on non-Indian-owned land. "Local-option" legislation passed by Congress allowed tribes to regulate liquor in Indian country, so long as state law was not violated. The Tribe's ordinance required a tribal license.

Issue: Was the congressional delegation of authority to the tribes valid?

Held: (1) The Indian Commerce Clause gives Congress the power to regulate alcohol sales to Indians "wherever situated."

(2) Tribes are "a good deal more than private, voluntary organizations."

(3) Congress' delegation was valid because it was to an entity possessing independent authority over the subject matter, based on the Tribe's "attributes of sovereignty."

(4) Under the holding of *Williams v. Lee,* the Tribe's authority could extend over non-Indians.

5. *Red Lake Band of Chippewa Indians v. Minnesota,* 248 N.W.2d 722 (Minn. 1976).

Facts: The Tribe enacted an extensive motor vehicle registration and licensing ordinance, and requested the State to extend reciprocity recognition and to grant exemptions from state licenses. The tribal ordinance was approved by the Secretary of the Interior.

Issue: Was the Tribe's regulatory jurisdiction over the reservation valid?

Held: (1) The State grants reciprocity and exemptions to other states and foreign countries. It should also grant the same to the Tribe, especially as the Tribe receives no payments from the State for maintenance of on-reservation roads, nor does the Tribe share in the State's license fees or gasoline taxes.

(2) There is no compelling state interest which justifies the State in imposing its licensing burden on the Tribe's self-government.

6. *United States v. Marcyes,* 557 F.2d 1361 (9th Cir. 1977).

Facts: Appellants were served with a restraining order, issued by a federal court, for selling fireworks on the Puyallup Reservation.

Issue: Did the Assimilative Crimes Act apply, incorporating Washington state law prohibiting fireworks?

Held: (1) Fireworks laws are "prohibitory rather than regulatory," designed "to promote the health and safety of all citizens."

(2) Although state regulatory laws may not be incorporated by the Assimilative Crimes Act, prohibitory state laws are.

(3) The Assimilative Crimes Act is "a general law of the United States, made applicable to Indian reservations by the General Crimes Act."

7. *Dry Creek Lodge, Inc. v. Arapahoe and Shoshone Tribes,* 623 F.2d 682 (10th Cir. 1980), *cert. denied,* 449 U.S. 1118 (1981).

Facts: A non-Indian owned land near a wilderness area. He built a lodge for hikers, but the Tribe closed an access road which crossed an allotment belonging to tribal members.

Issue: Did the Tribe violate the Indian Civil Rights Act? Was federal relief available?

Held: (1) The rule of *Santa Clara Pueblo v. Martinez* that tribal courts have exclusive jurisdiction for some matters arose from an entirely internal matter of tribal policy. No non-Indian property was involved. *Santa Clara Pueblo* also stressed the availability of tribal forums.

(2) The rule of *Santa Clara Pueblo* does not apply when tribal relief is unavailable, or if the matter is outside of internal tribal affairs and involves a non-Indian.

(3) "[T]he plaintiffs in this appeal have no remedy within the tribal machinery nor with the tribal officials in whose election they cannot participate. . . . There has to be a forum where the dispute can be settled," and federal relief is available.

8. *Seminole Tribe of Florida v. Butterworth,* 658 F.2d 310 (5th Cir. 1981), *cert. denied,* 455 U.S. 1020 (1982).

Facts: The Tribe operated a bingo hall on the reservation. The State, which had assumed Public Law 280 jurisdiction, threatened to arrest the Indian bingo operators for violation of state gambling laws.

Issue: Were the state gambling laws regulatory, rather than prohibitory, and thus outside the jurisdiction assumed under P.L. 280?

Held: (1) Under *Bryan v. Itasca County,* "states do not have general regulatory power" over Indians.

(2) The state bingo laws are regulatory--many exceptions to the bingo laws are permitted. The state law imposes regulations to avoid abuses.

(3) The rule in the *Colville* case, which required Indians to collect state taxes imposed on non-member cigarette buyers, does not apply here. In this case, the State's bingo laws would be enforced directly against the Indian operators.

9. *Montana v. United States,* 450 U.S. 544 (1981).

(*See* brief at IV.C.10)

10. *Confederated Salish and Kootenai Tribes v. Namen,* 665 F.2d 951 (9th Cir.), *cert. denied,* 459 U.S. 977 (1982).

Facts: The Tribes enacted an ordinance regulating the riparian rights of non-Indians owning land bordering navigable Flathead Lake within the Flathead Reservation.

Issue: Did the Tribes have regulatory authority to enact the ordinance?

Held: (1) Neither the 1904 Act opening the reservation to settlement, its legislative history, nor the circumstances surrounding its enactment "demonstrate that Congress intended the . . . Act to terminate the reservation."

(2) There is a strong presumption the United States held lands under navigable waterways for conveyance to future states. However, the Hell Gate Treaty of 1855 expressly "referred to the [Flathead] lake in defining the boundaries of the reservation." In addition, the dependence of the Kootenai Indians on fishing and the circumstances of the treaty ratification both indicate the existence of a "public exigency" surrounding the treaty and reservation. These factors confirm that the bed and banks of Flathead Lake are held in trust by the United States for the Tribes, and not owned by the State.

(3) Because the Tribes have beneficial title to the lake bed, "the Tribes are . . . seeking to regulate non-Indian use of tribal trust land, since the exercise by appellees of their riparian rights entails building . . . structures out onto the bed and banks of the south half of Flathead Lake."

(4) Use of the bed and banks of the lake could result in pollution, ecological damage, and affect treaty fishing rights. These all could "have the potential for significantly affecting the economy, welfare, and health of the Tribes." Thus, the Tribes had authority to regulate this non-Indian conduct.

11. *Knight v. Shoshone and Arapahoe Indian Tribes,* 670 F.2d 900 (10th Cir. 1982).

Facts: The Tribe enacted a zoning code, covering all land within the reservation (including non-Indian-owned fee lands). The Bureau of Indian Affairs indicated that the ordinance did not require its approval. Non-Indian developers planned to develop two ranches near Indian housing and ceremonial sites.

Issue: Did the Tribe have the authority to zone non-Indian lands within reservation boundaries?

Held: (1) Under the rule of *Montana v. United States,* " 'Indian tribes retain inherent sovereign power to exercise some forms of civil jurisdiction over non-Indians on their reservations, even on non-Indian fee lands,' " particularly where it relates to the " 'political integrity, the economic security or the health and welfare of the tribe.' "

(2) The Tribe's "inherent sovereign rights of self-government and territorial management" justify its efforts to maintain the "rural character" of the reservation.

12. *New Mexico v. Mescalero Apache Tribe,* 462 U.S. 333 (1983).
(*See* brief at IV.C.12)

13. *Rice v. Rehner,* 463 U.S. 713 (1983).

Facts: The State refused to grant a federally licensed Indian trader an exemption from state licensing laws for liquor sold on the reservation for off-premises consumption. The state license fee was $6,000, plus $409 per year.

Issue: Are state licensing laws preempted by federal regulation or statute?

Held: (1) There is no tradition of Indian sovereignty or inherent authority in "the narrow context" of liquor regulations. Rather, there is an "historical tradition of concurrent state and federal jurisdiction" over alcohol distribution in Indian country. There is no "single notion of tribal sovereignty" which applies to preemption analysis.

(2) Because there was no tradition of inherent tribal self-government over the liquor trade, the presumption of preemption of state law does not apply.

(3) 18 U.S.C. Section 1161 makes clear that Congress intended to delegate authority over reservation liquor transactions to both tribes (see *Mazurie*) and states. Although that statute does not expressly authorize the application of state regulatory laws over liquor transactions, the statutory language and the legislative history are "clear expressions of . . . congressional intent."

14. *United States v. Eberhardt,* 789 F.2d 1354 (9th Cir. 1986).
(*See* brief at IV.C.15)

15. *Northern Arapahoe Tribe v. Hodel,* 808 F.2d 741 (10th Cir. 1987).
(*See* brief at IV.C.16)

16. *California v. Cabazon Band of Mission Indians,* 480 U.S. 202 (1987).

Facts: The Cabazon and Morongo Bands of Mission Indians conduct gambling enterprises, including bingo and various card games, on their California reservations. The State of California attempted to stop the gambling pursuant to a California statute which prohibits bingo except for charitable purposes. Riverside County also became involved pursuant to local ordinances regulating bingo and prohibiting card game gambling. The Tribes filed suit in federal court to stop the State and County efforts.

Issue: Do the State and the County have the authority to regulate gambling on the Indian reservations?

Held: (1) Under Public Law 280, Congress granted California and other states broad criminal and civil jurisdiction over Indian country within the State. However, "it must be determined whether the law [to be applied] is criminal in nature, and thus fully applicable to the reservation . . . or civil in nature, and applicable only as it may be relevant to private civil litigation in state court."

(2) California argues that under its statute unregulated bingo is enforceable by criminal means, but that fact does not necessarily convert an otherwise regulatory law into a criminal law under P.L. 280.

(3) Because California does not prohibit all forms of gambling, its statute is regulatory in nature. Under the *Bryan v. Itasca County* rule, P.L. 280 does not authorize the application of state civil/regulatory laws on an Indian reservation. Because the County's ordinances are regulatory in nature, they also do not apply and the Court does not need to decide whether P.L. 280 authorizes the application of local ordinances to Indian reservations.

(4) Although California argues that the Organized Crime Control Act ("OCCA") authorizes the application of its gambling laws to Indian enterprises, the OCCA is a federal statute that says nothing about states having any involvement in enforcing federal crimes.

(5) "[T]he State's interest in preventing the infiltration of the tribal bingo enterprises by organized crime does not justify state regulation of the tribal bingo enterprises in light of the compelling federal and tribal interests [in Indian sovereignty and self-government, including tribal self-sufficiency and economic development] supporting them. State regulation would impermissibly infringe on tribal government. . . ."

17. *Brendale v. Confederated Tribes and Bands of the Yakima Indian Nation,* 492 U.S. ___, 106 L. Ed. 2d 342 (1989).

Facts: The Yakima Indian Reservation is divided into a "closed area," most of which is owned by the Yakima Tribe or its members and access to which is generally restricted to tribal members and permittees in order to preserve the natural, spiritual, and cultural values of the area, and an "open area," almost one-half of which is non-Indian-owned and to which access is not restricted. Brendale, a non-tribal-member owner of land in the closed area, and Wilkinson, a non-Indian owner of land in the open area, each received county approval for land developments that violated the Yakima Nation's zoning ordinance. The Yakima Nation filed separate actions in federal district court challenging the proposed developments and the County's exercise of zoning authority on the Reservation. The Yakima Nation asserted its own exclusive zoning authority over all Reservation land. After reviewing the three consolidated cases, the Supreme Court issued an unusual combination of opinions.

Issue: Does the Yakima Nation have exclusive authority to regulate land use within its reservation, regardless of land ownership?

Held: (1) Justice White, joined by Chief Justice Rehnquist, Justice Scalia and Justice Kennedy, interpret the Court's decision in *Montana* as "the tribe has no authority itself. . . to regulate the use of fee land." However, the Tribe does have a protectable interest when the use of reservation fee land is "demonstrably serious and must imperil the political integrity, economic security or the health and welfare of the tribe." The Tribe's interest arises under federal law, so "the Supremacy Clause requires state and local governments . . . to recognize and respect that interest in the course of their activities." Accordingly, the Tribe has no zoning authority over either the Brendale or Wilkinson property, but could have sued in federal court, particularly concerning the Brendale property, if Yakima County failed to respect the Tribe's interests.

(2) Justice Stevens and Justice O'Connor find that the Tribe's power to exclude nonmembers from its lands carries with it the power to define the essential character of the territory, in this case through zoning. Very little of the reservation's closed area is owned in fee, so the Tribe retains substantial power to exclude nonmembers and, accordingly, authority to regulate land use. Much of the land in the open area is fee land, and "it is unlikely that Congress intended to give the Tribe the power to determine the character of an area that is predominantly owned and populated by nonmembers, who represent 80 percent of the population yet lack a voice in tribal governance." Consequently, although the Tribe has the authority to zone the Brendale property, it does not have that authority regarding the Wilkinson property.

(3) Justice Blackmun, joined by Justice Brennan and Justice Marshall, finds that even under *Montana,* Indian "tribes may regulate the on-reservation conduct of non-Indians whenever a significant tribal interest is threatened or directly affected." Accordingly, "once the tribe's valid regulatory interest is established, the nature of land ownership does not diminish the tribe's inherent power to regulate in the area." Tribes have the uncontested power to regulate land use on trust land, and they have a significant interest in consistent and compatible land use on the reservation. It necessarily follows that Indian tribes retain zoning authority over non-Indian fee

lands on the reservation, and the Yakima Nation may regulate land use on both the Brendale and Wilkinson properties.

(4) By a 5 to 4 decision, the Yakima Nation retains the authority to regulate land use on the Brendale property within the closed area of the reservation. By a 6 to 3 decision, the Yakima Nation cannot regulate land use on the Wilkinson property in the open area.

3. Domestic Jurisdiction

Jurisdictional questions over domestic issues involving Indians arose infrequently in the courts until the last several decades. Public Law 280 allowed states to acquire jurisdiction. In the absence of Public Law 280 jurisdiction, however, courts have reacted consistently in Indian domestic matters. In the 1960 *Whyte v. District Court* case, an Indian woman filed for divorce from her Indian husband in state court, even though they had been married and were living on the reservation. The state court held that the tribal court had exclusive jurisdiction. When one of the parties is non-Indian, however, state courts tend to accept jurisdiction.

Custody and adoption of Indian children has been one area that state courts have been reluctant to enter. The *Wakefield v. Little Light* court in 1975 found that state court interference with tribal jurisdiction over the custody of Indian children constituted an inappropriate infringement on tribal self-government, particularly when the child was domiciled on the reservation. However, when the Indian mother and child were not domiciled on the reservation, and the mother had consented to the adoption, the court in the 1977 *In Re Adoption of Roe* case held that the state court had jurisdiction.

Most Indian custody and adoption issues now are resolved in favor of tribal jurisdiction under the 1978 Indian Child Welfare Act (ICWA). In the case of Indian children who are domiciled off a reservation, states have concurrent jurisdiction over adoption and custody. Even then, if foster care placement or termination of parental rights are involved, the case must be transferred to tribal court upon the request of either parent, the Indian custodian, or the tribe. Such transfer may be declined if the state finds "good cause" to so decline, or if the tribal court itself declines the transfer, or if either parent objects to the transfer. Constitutionality of the ICWA was upheld in 1980 as being based on the political relationship between Indian tribes and the United States, not violative of equal protection or due process guarantees, according to *In Re Guardianship of D.L.L. and C.L.L.*

1. *Whyte v. District Court,* 140 Colo. 334, 346 P.2d 1012 (1959), *cert. denied,* 363 U.S. 829 (1960).

Facts: An Indian woman filed for divorce in state court. Her husband was also an Indian, and they were married and domiciled on the Ute Mountain Reservation.

Issue: Did the state court have subject matter jurisdiction over the divorce?

Held: (1) Under *Williams v. Lee,* "a contract of marriage entered into on an Indian reservation between two enrolled members of the tribe must be governed by tribal law," and the tribal court has exclusive jurisdiction.

(2) The State had not assumed P.L. 280 jurisdiction and Congress had not otherwise authorized state jurisdiction.

2. *Bad Horse v. Bad Horse,* 163 Mont. 445, 517 P.2d 893, *cert. denied,* 419 U.S. 847 (1974).

Facts: An Indian couple was married off the reservation under state law. The husband later sought a divorce in state court; the wife was served with process on the reservation. The Tribe had passed a resolution in 1937 leaving domestic relations to state law.

Issue: Did the state court have subject matter jurisdiction over the divorce?

Held: (1) There is no interference with tribal government because the Tribe does not exercise jurisdiction over marriage and divorce, no non-Indian parties are infringing on tribal government, and the marriage took place off the reservation under state law.

(2) Service of process on an Indian defendant within the reservation was proper to effectuate the state court's jurisdiction over the subject matter.

Note: *Bad Horse* has since been overruled by the Montana Supreme Court, based on a tribal court opinion which held that the Tribe had exclusive jurisdiction over the Tribe's domestic relations.

3. *Wakefield v. Little Light,* 276 Md. 333, 347 A.2d 228 (1975).

Facts: A non-Indian couple sought to adopt a Crow Indian child in Maryland state court. The child's mother and the Tribe objected and sought return of the child to the reservation. The mother had previously given consent to the non-Indian couple to take the child off the reservation and to their being appointed as guardians under state law. The tribal court had made the child a ward of the court and appointed the couple guardians for one year. The child had lived in Maryland for seven months and was enrolled in Maryland schools.

Issue: Did the Maryland courts have subject matter jurisdiction?

Held: (1) "There can be no greater threat to 'essential tribal relations' and no greater infringement on the right of the Crow Tribe to govern themselves than to interfere with tribal control over the custody of their children."

(2) The child's domicile was on the reservation, so the State lacked jurisdiction.

4. *In Re Adoption of Doe,* 89 N.M. 606, 555 P.2d 906, *cert. denied,* 558 P.2d 619 (1976).

Facts: A non-Indian couple sought to adopt a Navajo child in state court. The mother consented to the adoption, but her father (the child's grandfather) sought custody. The child neither resided nor was domiciled on the reservation.

Issue: Did the state court have subject matter jurisdiction?

Held: (1) "Whatever concurrent jurisdiction the courts of the Navajo Nation might have, New Mexico had an interest in the welfare of the child who was in New Mexico and not within the boundaries of the reservation." Thus, the state court had jurisdiction.

(2) Cases supporting exclusive tribal jurisdiction are those "where the child was a resident of or domiciled on an Indian reservation."

5. *Francisco v. State,* 113 Ariz. 427, 556 P.2d 1 (1976).

Facts: A paternity suit was brought in state court against an Indian. The defendant was served by the county sheriff on the reservation. The baby was born off the reservation to an Indian mother.

Issue: Did the state court have personal jurisdiction over defendant?

Held: (1) There was no personal jurisdiction due to invalid service of process, because the state laws applying to service by the sheriff "could not be applied to an Indian while on the reservation."

(2) The state court did have subject matter jurisdiction, and "service of process could have validly been effected through the Papago Indian authorities . . . pursuant to tribal laws."

6. *Fisher v. District Court,* 424 U.S. 382 (1976).

Facts: An Indian sought to adopt an Indian child in state court. The child was a ward of the tribal court, and all of the relevant parties (the petitioner, the child, and the child's parents) were tribal members residing on the Northern Cheyenne Reservation.

Issue: Did the Montana state courts have subject matter jurisdiction over the adoption proceeding?

Held: (1) "Since the adoption proceeding [arose] on the Indian reservation, the jurisdiction of the Tribal Court is exclusive."

(2) State court jurisdiction "would interfere with the powers of self-government" of the Tribe, under the *Williams v. Lee* test.

(3) Denying the adopting parents access to state court is not racial discrimination. The tribal court's exclusive jurisdiction derives "from the quasi-sovereign status" of the Tribe.

7. *In Re Guardianship of D.L.L. and C.L.L.,* 291 N.W.2d 278 (S.D. 1980).

Facts: Indian children were placed in temporary custody of a non-Indian group foster home, pursuant to an order of the tribal court and with the parents' consent. When the tribal court later ordered the children returned to the parents, the foster home refused and sought guardianship in South Dakota State Court.

Issue: Did the state court have subject matter jurisdiction? Was the Indian Child Welfare Act of 1978 (ICWA) valid?

Held: (1) Congress' plenary power, derived from the Indian Commerce Clause of the Constitution, supports the constitutionality of the ICWA against petitioner's claim that it violates the Tenth Amendment (reserving non-delegated powers to the states or the people).

(2) Due process and equal protection are not violated because the ICWA makes its distinctions based on the political relationship between the tribes and the United States, not on racial discrimination.

(3) The children were wards of the tribal court and domiciliaries of the reservation (where their parents resided). Thus, tribal court jurisdiction was exclusive.

8. *In the Matter of the Appeal in Pima County Juvenile Action No. S-903,* 130 Ariz. 202, 635 P.2d 187 (1981), *cert. denied,* 455 U.S. 1007 (1982).

Facts: An Indian mother consented to adoptive placement of her child, but later withdrew it before the adoption had become final. The adopting parents objected and sought a state court order terminating parental rights. The Tribe and the Indian parent requested transfer to tribal court.

Issue: Did the state court have jurisdiction under the Indian Child Welfare Act (ICWA)?

Held: (1) The Tribe had exclusive jurisdiction, because the mother was domiciled on the reservation and the child retained the domicile of its mother.

(2) There was not "good cause" for the State to retain jurisdiction even if it had concurrent jurisdiction. The mother's fitness could best be determined on the reservation. The ICWA states that when consent to adoption is timely withdrawn, "the child shall be returned."

(3) No rehabilitative programs were undertaken, and the mother's fitness was not refuted "beyond a reasonable doubt." Thus, termination of parental rights was not permissible.

9. *Mississippi Band of Choctaw Indians v. Holyfield*, 490 U.S. ___, 104 L. Ed. 2d 26 (1989).

Facts: Unmarried Indian parents, both domiciliaries of the reservation, voluntarily consented to the adoption of their two children by a non-Indian couple. The children had been born off the reservation and had never resided there. The state court granted custody to the non-Indian couple, and the Tribe objected to state jurisdiction.

Issue: Did the state court have jurisdiction under the Indian Child Welfare Act (ICWA)?

Held: (1) "Section 1911(a) [of the ICWA] establishes exclusive jurisdiction in the tribal courts for proceedings concerning an Indian child 'who resides or is domiciled within the reservation of such tribe,' as well as for wards of tribal courts regardless of domicile. Section 1911(b) . . . creates concurrent but presumptively tribal jurisdiction in the case of children not domiciled on the reservation: on petition of either parent or the tribe, state-court proceedings for foster care placement or termination of parental rights are to be transferred to the tribal court, except in cases of 'good cause,' objection by either parent, or declination of jurisdiction by the tribal court."

(2) 25 U.S.C. § 1915(a), "absent 'good cause' to the contrary, mandates that adoptive placements be made preferentially with (1) members of the child's extended family, (2) other members of the same tribe, or (3) other Indian families."

(3) "The sole issue in this case is . . . whether the twins were 'domiciled' on the reservation."

(4) Congress intended the Court to apply a uniform federal law of domicile under the ICWA, and the Court will apply common-law principles of domicile not inconsistent with the policy of the ICWA. The domicile of minors is determined by the domicile of their parents, and for illegitimate children that means the domicile of the mother. In this case, the mother's domicile was on the reservation. "Thus, it is clear that at their birth the twin babies were also domiciled on the reservation, even though they themselves had never been there." The Tribe had jurisdiction, despite the voluntary consent of their parents.

B. Criminal Jurisdiction

Federal legislation has had far-reaching effects over criminal matters in Indian country. The General Crimes Act of 1817, also called the Federal Enclaves Act, extended to Indian country "the general laws of the United States as to the punishment of offenses" which are applicable in areas under federal jurisdiction. Exceptions included crimes by an Indian against another Indian, crimes committed by an Indian who has been punished under tribal law, and treaty stipulations. The effect of the General Crimes Act was to provide for prosecution of crimes by non-Indians against Indians, and of non-major crimes by Indians against non-Indians, where the crime was committed in Indian country.

Deficiencies in the General Crimes Act were made clear in *Ex Parte Crow Dog* in 1883. The Supreme Court concluded that since the Act excluded crimes of Indians against other Indians, the United States had no authority to prosecute the Indian plaintiff for murdering another tribal member. This problem was quickly remedied by Congress. The Major Crimes Act of 1885 today lists fourteen crimes which, when committed by an Indian in Indian country, result in federal prosecutorial jurisdiction. This jurisdiction applies whether the victim was Indian or non-Indian. Tribes exercise concurrent jurisdiction over these offenses, due to inherent tribal sovereignty, but the Indian Civil Rights Act of 1968 resulted in a practical limitation of tribal criminal jurisdiction to minor offenses, punishable by a maximum $500 fine or six months' imprisonment.

States retain exclusive jurisdiction over crimes by non-Indians against other non-Indians in Indian country. Public Law 280 extends general criminal jurisdiction over *all* crimes committed in Indian country to those states to which it applies. Otherwise, tribal criminal jurisdiction is exclusive for non-major crimes committed by Indians against Indians in Indian country. Tribes also retain concurrent jurisdiction (with the federal government) over non-major crimes committed by Indians against non-Indians in Indian country. But, the Supreme Court held in 1978 in *Oliphant v. Suquamish Tribe* that tribes have no criminal jurisdiction over non-Indians.

1. *United States v. McBratney,* 104 U.S. 621 (1881).

Facts: One white man murdered another on the Ute Reservation in Colorado. A federal court convicted him.

Issue: Did the federal court have jurisdiction?

Held: Colorado entered the Union on an "equal footing" with the other states, which meant that it "acquired" criminal jurisdiction over its own citizens and other white persons throughout the whole of the territory within its limits, including the Ute Reservation.

2. *Ex Parte Crow Dog,* 109 U.S. 556 (1883).

Facts: A Sioux Indian murdered another member of the Tribe on the reservation. The federal court sentenced him to death under the terms of the 1868 Treaty.

Issue: Did the federal court have jurisdiction?

Held: (1) The General Crimes Act excepts crimes "committed by one Indian against the person or property of another."

(2) The 1868 Treaty subjected the Sioux to federal jurisdiction for crimes against whites or blacks or Indians of another tribe, but not for crimes against another tribal member.

(3) Congress did not clearly express its intention to extend the "external and unknown code" of white morality over the Sioux. Thus, the federal "conviction and sentence are void, and . . . his imprisonment is illegal."

3. *Keeble v. United States,* 412 U.S. 205 (1973).

Facts: An Indian was prosecuted in federal court for assault with intent to commit serious bodily injury on another Indian on the Crow Creek Reservation. The Court refused to instruct the jury that it might find the defendant guilty of the lesser included offense of simple assault.

Issue: Did the Major Crimes Act's enumeration of certain crimes prohibit federal court jurisdiction over a lesser included offense which was not itself among the enumerated crimes?

Held: (1) Under the Major Crimes Act Indians are entitled to be tried "in the same manner" as other persons committing the same crime. This includes the benefit of a jury instruction on lesser included offenses.

(2) To preclude a jury instruction on a lesser included offense in a Major Crimes Act case "would raise serious constitutional questions" under the Due Process Clause.

4. *United States v. Antelope*, 430 U.S. 641 (1977).

Facts: Indian defendants were convicted under the Major Crimes Act for murder, as defined in the federal felony-murder statute. If they had been non-Indians, tried for murder committed on the reservation under state law, the prosecution would have had to prove premeditation and deliberation, because the State did not have a felony-murder statute.

Issue: Did the different treatment of Indians and non-Indians violate due process, in the form of racial discrimination?

Held: (1) Federal legislation with respect to Indian tribes is "not based upon impermissible racial classifications." Rather, it is based upon the Constitution and the history of the federal-tribal political relationship.

(2) Due process was not violated, because the federal law was "evenhanded."

5. *Oliphant v. Suquamish Indian Tribe*, 435 U.S. 191 (1978).

Facts: Non-Indian petitioners were arraigned in tribal court for offenses in violation of the tribal code taking place on the reservation. The reservation was a heavily checkerboarded area, with a majority non-Indian population.

Issue: Do tribes have inherent authority to assert jurisdiction over non-Indians who commit offenses on the reservation?

Held: (1) Indian treaties "cannot be interpreted in isolation but must be read in light of the common notions of the day and the assumptions of those who drafted them."

(2) Tribes' retained powers are limited by treaties, statutes, and by their status as domestic dependent nations.

(3) Tribes have no power to transfer lands to whomever they please or to exercise external political sovereignty. It is inconsistent with their status to try non-Indians.

(4) Congress could delegate such powers to tribes by statute. Since this has not yet been done, "Indian tribes do not have inherent jurisdiction to try and punish non-Indians."

6. *United States v. Wheeler,* 435 U.S. 313 (1978).

Facts: An Indian defendant was sentenced in tribal court for disorderly conduct and contributing to the delinquency of a minor. A year later, he was indicted in federal court, under the Major Crimes Act, for rape arising out of the same incident.

Issue: Did the Fifth Amendment's Double Jeopardy Clause bar the federal prosecution, after the tribal court conviction on the lesser included offense? Are tribes "arms of the federal government"?

Held: (1) States and the national government are separate sovereigns, and federal prosecution does not bar subsequent state prosecution for the same acts. By one act, the offender commits two offenses.

(2) Similarly, "Indian tribes still possess those aspects of sovereignty not withdrawn by treaty or statute, or by implication as a necessary result of their dependent status." A tribe's prosecution "of its own members" is an exercise of its "retained sovereignty."

7. *United States v. John,* 437 U.S. 634 (1978).

Facts: Defendant was indicted under the Major Crimes Act for assault with intent to kill. The United States Court of Appeals ruled that the federal courts lacked jurisdiction because Choctaw lands in Mississippi were not "Indian country." Defendant was then tried and convicted in state court.

Issue: Is the Choctaw country in Mississippi "Indian country"?

Held: (1) Although the federal government attempted to remove all Choctaws to west of the Mississippi River, those who remained behind were still "Indian."

(2) The federal government had a long course of dealing with the Mississippi Choctaw after removal, including the purchase of lands in 1918, inclusion in the Indian Reorganization Act of 1934, and a proclamation of a reservation in 1944. Thus, the Choctaw lands were "Indian country."

(3) There was a basis for federal prosecution, and the State does not have that power.

8. *Solem v. Bartlett,* 465 U.S. 463 (1983).

Facts: An Indian was convicted of attempted rape in state court. The crime took place in a part of the reservation that was opened to settlement by Congress. Two-thirds of the tribal members lived in these opened areas, and the tribal government was located there. Few white homesteaders settled there. The Bureau of Indian Affairs maintained responsibility for the area.

Issue: Did the legislation opening the reservation diminish it, so that the State had criminal jurisdiction in the opened areas?

Held: (1) "Only Congress can divest a reservation of its lands and diminish its boundaries. . . . Diminishment . . . will not be lightly inferred."

(2) In determining congressional intent, the Court looks to the statutory language in the legislation opening the lands (was there language of cession?) and to the events surrounding the passage of the Act and subsequent events (including the Bureau of Indian Affairs' activities and the number of non-Indians who entered the open areas).

(3) Language of cession buttressed by a congressional commitment to compensate the Tribe for its opened land creates "an almost insurmountable presumption that Congress meant for the tribe's reservation to be diminished."

(4) In that there was no language of cession; only "a few isolated and ambiguous" references to cession in the legislative history; no clear governmental approach in the years following the opening of the lands; and a continuing "strong tribal presence in the opened areas," the Court refused to upset "the presumption that Congress did not intend to diminish the Reservation."

9. *Duro v. Reina,* 58 U.S.L.W. 4643 (U.S. May 29, 1990).

Facts: Duro, a non-member Indian living on the Salt River Indian Reservation, allegedly shot and killed another non-member Indian while they were both on the Reservation. A criminal complaint was filed against Duro in tribal court charging him with discharging a firearm within reservation boundaries. The tribal court denied Duro's motion to dismiss for lack of criminal jurisdiction, and Duro petitioned the federal district court for a writ of habeas corpus and/or a writ of prohibition.

Issue: Does a tribal court have criminal jurisdiction over a non-member Indian accused of committing a crime against another non-member Indian on the Tribe's reservation?

Held: (1) "The retained sovereignty of the tribes is that needed to control their own internal relations, and to preserve their own unique customs and social order . . . . [including] [t]he power of a tribe to prescribe and enforce rules of conduct for its own members. . . ."

(2) "[Indian] tribes are not mere fungible groups of homogeneous persons among whom any Indian would feel at home. . . . Petitioner's general status as an Indian says little about his consent to the exercise of authority over him by a particular tribe."

(3) "For purposes of criminal jurisdiction, petitioner's relations with this Tribe are the same as the non-Indians in *Oliphant.* We hold that the Tribe's powers over him are subject to the same limitations."

C. Tax Jurisdiction

Taxation issues, including special exemptions and the power to levy taxes, reveal the unique status of Indian tribes and their property, and this status is based in federal statutes and treaties. In 1956, the Supreme Court determined in *Squire v. Capoeman* that the General Allotment Act exempted Indian allotments and income derived therefrom from all taxes, until a fee patent is issued for the property. The same effect resulted for tribal reservation property and income with regard to state income taxes in the 1973 *McClanahan v. Arizona State Tax Commission* case, but on different theories. The Court held that various federal laws and treaties preempted the state taxes, and that the taxes infringed on tribal self-government. Even jurisdiction conferred by Public Law 280 does not overcome this barrier to state taxation, according to *Bryan v. Itasca County.*

State taxes on non-Indian activities on the reservation also are precluded if comprehensive federal regulations preempt them. The Supreme Court in *Warren Trading Post v. Arizona Tax Commissioner* found such preemption regarding a retail trading business. More recently, both a logging company's highway activities and a construction company's school construction work were exempted from preempted state taxes. However, if the activity is not federally regulated, *Moe v. Confederated Salish and Kootenai Tribes* decided that states can tax sales to non-Indians and make the Indian sellers collect the tax. States can even tax non-Indian lessees of Indian property, since the tax falls on the lessee and not the Indian owners or their property.

Tribal authority to levy taxes on non-Indians has been the subject of much recent controversy. In 1980 the Supreme Court decided *Washington v. Confederated Tribes of the Colville Reservation,* which not only allowed state sales taxes on non-Indian purchases of cigarettes on the reservation, but also recognized concurrent tribal authority to tax those same sales.

More recently in *Merrion v. Jicarilla Apache Tribe,* the Court upheld the Tribe's oil and gas severance tax on non-Indian companies. It based its reasoning on the Tribe's power to exclude non-members from the reservation and the Tribe's inherent power as a government to tax revenues generated on the reservation, particularly when the taxpayer benefits from tribal services. In addition to these considerations, the Jicarilla Apache Tribe followed their tribal constitution, adopted under the Indian Reorganization Act (IRA), by having the Secretary of the Interior approve the taxation ordinance.

Most recently, in 1985 the Court decided the similar *Kerr-McGee v. Navajo Tribe* case even more broadly. Because the Navajo Tribe had not adopted the IRA, there was no statutory obligation that the federal government approve taxes on reservation mining activities. The Tribe's inherent power to tax also was not preempted by federal regulation of mining leases.

Although tribes have received a mixed reception from the courts in many areas of governmental jurisdiction, recognition of their power to tax non-Indians on the reservation has now been well-established. How far this power extends will, no doubt, be the subject of substantial future litigation.

1. *Squire v. Capoeman,* 351 U.S. 1 (1956).

Facts: The Bureau of Indian Affairs sold timber on an Indian's allotted land, netting the allottee substantial income.

Issue: Was the income subject to federal income tax?

Held: (1) The General Allotment Act, as construed in favor of Indians, promised eventually to transfer the fee title of the allotment "free of all charge or encumbrance whatsoever." Until such time as a fee patent is issued, the allotment and income derived from it are to be "free from all taxes."

(2) Although Indians are ordinarily subject to federal income tax "as are other citizens," an exemption is made when treaties or remedial legislation requires.

2. *Warren Trading Post v. Arizona Tax Commission,* 380 U.S. 685 (1965).

Facts: Appellant operated a retail trading business with Indians on the Navajo Reservation, under a federal license. The State levied a "gross income tax" on the business.

Issue: Is state taxation preempted by comprehensive federal statutes and regulations?

Held: The "all-inclusive regulations and the statutes authorizing them" show that "Congress has taken the business of Indian trading on reservations so fully in hand that no room remains for state laws imposing additional burdens upon traders."

3. *McClanahan v. Arizona State Tax Commission*, 411 U.S. 164 (1973).

Facts: An employer withheld an amount of money from an Indian's wages to cover the state income tax. The employee was a member of the Tribe, living on the reservation, and all income was earned on the reservation.

Issue: Is the state tax barred by the *Williams v. Lee* "infringement test"? Is the state tax preempted by federal treaties and statutes?

Held: (1) "[T]he trend has been away from the idea of inherent Indian sovereignty as a bar to state jurisdiction and toward reliance on federal pre-emption." "The Indian sovereignty doctrine is relevant . . . but because it provides a backdrop against which the applicable treaties and federal statutes must be read."

(2) The Navajo Treaty, the Arizona Enabling Act, the Buck Act, and P.L. 280 all point to a congressional "intent to maintain the tax exempt status of reservation Indians."

(3) The *Williams* "infringement test" deals "principally with situations involving non-Indians." Where only reservation Indians and activities are involved, the federal laws may not be "ignored simply because tribal self-government has not been infringed." In any event, the rights of "reservation Indians" were infringed by the tax in this case.

4. *Mescalero Apache Tribe v. Jones*, 411 U.S. 145 (1973).

Facts: The State assessed a gross receipts tax on a tribally owned, off-reservation ski resort. The State also assessed a use tax based on the price of materials to construct two ski lifts.

Issue: Were the state taxes permissible?

Held: (1) *McClanahan* makes clear that taxing "reservation lands or Indian income from activities carried on within the boundaries of the reservation . . . is not permissible absent congressional consent."

(2) But, "absent express federal laws to the contrary, Indians going beyond reservation boundaries have generally been held subject to nondiscriminatory state law" (e.g. criminal laws, fishing, taxation). The New Mexico Enabling Act permits such taxation of Indian off-reservation income, and nothing in the Indian Reorganization Act prohibits tax on off-reservation income "simply because the land from which it derived . . . is itself exempt from tax."

(3) The ski lifts, however, were permanently attached to the realty, so a tax upon use of those materials would be a tax on the land itself, which is prohibited.

5. *Moe v. Confederated Salish and Kootenai Tribes of the Flathead Indian Reservation*, 425 U.S. 463 (1976).

Facts: The State imposed a personal property tax on Indians' on-reservation property; a vendor license fee on an Indian conducting a tribal cigarette business on-reservation; and a cigarette sales tax to be applied to on-reservation sales by Indians.

Issue: Were the state taxes preempted by congressional statutes, as read against the backdrop of the Indian sovereignty doctrine?

Held: (1) *McClanahan* cannot be distinguished on the ground that the Salish and Kootenai Tribes, unlike the Navajo Tribe, "are now so completely integrated with the non-Indians . . . that there is no longer any reason to accord them different treatment than other citizens."

(2) The General Allotment Act did not extend state jurisdiction to fee-owned lands within the reservation.

(3) Indian tax immunity does not constitute invidious racial discrimination in violation of due process, under the *Morton v. Mancari* rule.

(4) The tax on sales to non-Indians on the reservation actually falls on the non-Indians. The Indian seller merely collects the tax for the State. This is a "minimal burden" on tribal self-government, and "not, strictly speaking, a tax at all" on Indians.

(5) The other taxes and licensing requirements are in conflict with congressional statutes, including the cigarette sales tax on on-reservation sales by Indians to Indians.

6. *Bryan v. Itasca County*, 426 U.S. 373 (1976).

Facts: An Indian's mobile home on the reservation gave rise to a county personal property tax. The State was a Public Law 280 state.

Issue: Did the State's assumption of civil jurisdiction under P.L. 280 extend to general regulatory control over reservations, including taxation?

Held: (1) The rules of *McClanahan* and *Moe* preclude the county from levying a personal property tax on a reservation Indian without congressional consent.

(2) P.L. 280's grant of civil jurisdiction was primarily intended to

cover "private civil litigation involving reservation Indians in state court."

(3) "There is notably absent any conferral of state jurisdiction over tribes themselves."

(4) Tribes retain extensive regulatory powers over the reservation even after P.L. 280.

(5) The statute is construed liberally, with "doubtful expressions being resolved in favor of the Indians," and Congress' present policy of "strengthening tribal self-government" taken into account.

7. *Fort Mojave Tribe v. County of San Bernardino*, 543 F.2d 1253 (9th Cir. 1976), *cert. denied*, 430 U.S. 983 (1977).

Facts: The reservation was located within three states, one of which (California) imposed "possessory interest" tax on the lessees of trust property. The Tribe had its own possessory interest tax. The Tribe had 99-year leases with non-Indian lessees for development.

Issue: Were the state taxes preempted under the rule of *McClanahan*? Did they infringe on tribal self-government under the *Williams v. Lee* holding?

Held: (1) The Indian Reorganization Act's prohibition against "encumbrances" on tribal lands or other assets did not apply to these taxes, because the "legal incidence of the tax . . . falls on the lessee."

(2) P.L. 280 "neither precludes nor authorizes" such taxes.

(3) Although there may be an economic burden on the Tribe as a result of the state taxes (in the form of reduced revenues from the leases), "no Indian or Indian land is being subjected to direct state court process." Hence, tribal self-government is not interfered with.

(4) Under federal law, the Secretary of the Interior can "thwart tax sales." California has other methods of enforcing its taxes against non-Indians.

8. *Washington v. Confederated Tribes of the Colville Indian Reservation*, 447 U.S. 134 (1980).

Facts: The State enforced a cigarette excise tax and a sales tax against non-members of the Tribes who purchased cigarettes on-reservation. The Tribes had their own extensive schemes for regulating and taxing on-reservation cigarette sales, and tribal taxes generated significant revenue. Purchasers could save a dollar per carton of cigarettes.

Issue: Was the state tax on on-reservation sales to non-members valid? Could the State require the on-reservation seller to collect the tax?

Held: (1) The Tribes' tax on non-members was valid. "Indian tribes possess a broad measure of civil jurisdiction over the activities of non-Indians on Indian reservation lands in which the tribes have a significant interest." The *Oliphant* decision does not change this.

(2) The State's taxes are not preempted by federal law. The cigarette sales have "no substantial connection to reservation lands," and federal Indian law does not "authorize Indian tribes thus to market an exemption from state taxation to persons who would normally do their business elsewhere."

(3) The State is not required to give a credit for the tribal taxes paid.

(4) "For most practical purposes, [non-member] Indians stand on the same footing as non-Indians resident on the reservation." Thus, the state tax can apply to sales to them.

9. *White Mountain Apache Tribe v. Bracker,* 448 U.S. 136 (1980).

Facts: The Tribe contracted with a logging company to assist with the tribal timber harvest. The State imposed a "motor carrier license tax" and a "use fuel tax" on the logging company's highway activities, even though these logging activities took place on Bureau of Indian Affairs or tribal roads within the reservation.

Issue: Was the state tax preempted by federal law, or did it infringe on tribal self-government?

Held: (1) There are "two independent but related barriers to the assertion of state regulatory authority over tribal reservations and members": federal preemption and infringement on tribal self-government.

(2) "Ambiguities in federal law have been construed generously in order to comport with . . . traditional notions of sovereignty and with the federal policy of encouraging tribal independence."

(3) In view of the federal government's extensive regulation of Indian timber harvesting and Bureau of Indian Affairs roads, "there is no room for [state] taxes in the comprehensive federal scheme."

10. *Ramah Navajo School Board v. Bureau of Revenue,* 458 U.S. 832 (1982).

Facts: The Tribe established an Indian school board and contracted with the Bureau of Indian Affairs to hire a construction company for a new school on the reservation. The State imposed a gross receipts tax on the non-Indian contractor.

Issue: Was the state tax "preempted by federal law," or did it "interfere with the Tribe's ability to exercise its sovereign functions"?

Held: (1) "Federal regulation of the construction and financing of Indian education institutions" is so pervasive as to leave "no room for the additional burden" of state taxation on the contractor.

(2) The State's mere "desire to increase revenues" is not enough of a state interest to justify interference with a comprehensive federal scheme.

11. *Merrion v. Jicarilla Apache Tribe,* 455 U.S. 130 (1982).

Facts: The Tribe, which had accepted reorganization under the Indian Reorganization Act and whose constitution empowered it, with approval of the Interior Secretary, to tax non-members, imposed a severance tax on oil and gas sold or transported off the reservation by a long-term, non-Indian lessee, pursuant to an ordinance approved by the Secretary.

Issue: Was the tax valid? Did it violate the Commerce Clause of the Constitution?

Held: (1) Under the holding of *Colville,* "the power to tax is an essential attribute of Indian sovereignty because it is a necessary instrument of self-government and territorial management." This power "does not simply derive from the Tribe's power to exclude . . . but is an inherent power. . . ."

(2) The Tribe's power to tax non-members is "strongest when the revenues are derived from value generated on the reservation by activities involving the Tribe and when the taxpayer is the recipient of tribal services."

(3) Alternatively, the Tribe's power to exclude would itself justify the tax, even though the tax was not mentioned in the original lease.

(4) The Tribe's tax does not violate the Commerce Clause. Minerals sold on the reservation and those transported away are taxed in the same manner. Moreover, Congress and the Secretary of the Interior have approved the tribal tax.

12. *Kerr-McGee Corp. v. Navajo Tribe of Indians,* 471 U.S. 195 (1985).

Facts: The Navajo Tribal Council enacted two business tax ordinances, taxing the value of leasehold interests and the receipts from sale of property from or services within those lands. The ordinances were submitted to the Bureau of Indian Affairs, who informed the Tribe that Department of the Interior review and approval was not required. Kerr-McGee held substantial federally approved leaseholds on the reservation. Kerr-McGee alleged that the tribal taxing ordinances were invalid without the approval of the Secretary of the Interior.

Issue: Were the tribal taxing ordinances valid, as applied to non-members of the Tribe?

Held: (1) The Indian Reorganization Act of 1934 (IRA) authorizes tribes to adopt a constitution with the approval of the Secretary, and "[m]any tribal constitutions written under the IRA . . . called for Secretarial approval of tax laws affecting non-Indians." However, "the terms of the IRA do not govern tribes, like the Navajo, which declined to accept its provisions."

(2) "Nor do we agree that Congress intended to recognize as legitimate only those tribal taxes authorized by constitutions written under the IRA."

(3) The authority of the Secretary to regulate Indian mineral leasing under the Indian Mineral Leasing Act of 1938 does not include review of tribal taxes on mineral production.

(4) "The power to tax members and non-members alike is surely an essential attribute" of tribal self-government.

13. *Oklahoma Tax Commission v. Graham,* 489 U.S. ___, 103 L. Ed. 2d 924 (1989).

Facts: The Chickasaw Nation conducted bingo games and sold cigarettes at a motel it owned and operated in the State of Oklahoma. The State filed a complaint in state court to collect unpaid taxes on the cigarettes and games receipts. The Tribe removed the case from state court to federal district court, asserting federal question jurisdiction. The State moved to remand. The district court dismissed the case, holding it was barred by tribal sovereign immunity.

Issue: Is tribal sovereign immunity an implicit federal question in a suit against a tribe in state court, making removal to federal court possible?

Held: (1) Unless Congress provides otherwise, "a case is not properly removed to federal court unless it might have been brought there originally."

(2) In this case, the only asserted basis for federal jurisdiction is the presence of a federal question, which is governed by the "well-pleaded complaint" rule. Jurisdiction must be determined from

the plaintiff's statement of the claim, without consideration of anticipated defenses.

(3) "The possible existence of a tribal immunity defense . . . did not convert Oklahoma tax claims into federal questions, and there was no independent basis for original federal jurisdiction to support removal." Accordingly, the case was improperly removed from the Oklahoma state courts.

IV. INDIAN RESERVED RIGHTS

The United States entered into treaties with the Indians to secure vast expanses of Indian land for non-Indian settlement. These treaties, and later executive orders, usually confined the Indians to geographically defined reservations, where they were to maintain themselves, learn the "arts of civilization," and prepare themselves for entry and assimilation into non-Indian society. As long as the non-Indian population was able to fill up the former Indian land without direct confrontation with the Indians, few questions arose over the treaties. But when population pressures and economic interests conflicted with Indian perceptions of the rights they reserved for themselves in treaties, the courts were called upon to resolve the issues. These same conflicts continue today.

Early court cases provided fundamental treaty interpretations. *Worchester v. Georgia* set the standard for interpreting treaties in favor of the Indian signatories; both *Ward v. Racehorse* and *United States v. Winans* addressed the nature of specifically reserved treaty rights as property interests; and *Winters v. United States* found implied Indian water rights sufficient to fulfill the purposes of the reservation. Later, as government Indian policies changed and the national economy touched Indian lands, the focus of the judicial conflicts shifted.

Indian allotment acts raised questions about the rights of Indian allottees and their non-Indian successors. *United States v. Hibner* typifies the view of allottees as private landowners capable of transferring property interests. *United States v. Shoshone Tribe* discussed the nature of Indian occupancy in terms of reservation natural resources, and the Supreme Court found little real difference between that occupancy and fee simple title. Stricter interpretations of treaty language and more rigid requirements for compensation for the taking of Indian property characterized America's entry into the Termination Era. *Menominee Tribe v. United States* closed out the era with a finding that some treaty rights can survive termination.

Recent cases frequently arise out of the fundamental struggle between Indian tribes and states as competing governmental entities. Although these cases usually focus on more refined interpretations of specific treaty language, they reflect the underlying conflict. Water adjudication and hunting and fishing rights are indicative of the struggle for jurisdiction. Although Indian tribes generally have been successful with hunting and fishing, states share concurrent jurisdiction with the federal government over water rights. Conflicts over lands and resources produced judicial holdings that resulted in diminishment of Indian lands and some weakening of tribal jurisdiction generally. Overall, the trend has been toward more specific definition and restriction of Indian rights, lands, and jurisdiction. However, on some issues, notably hunting and fishing and water rights, the courts continue to support Indian treaties and tribal sovereignty.

A. Indian Treaties

Indian treaties and executive orders and agreements still, more than one hundred years after the last treaty was signed, determine the rights of Indians today. These documents, contracts between the United States government and Indian tribes, were the mechanism whereby many tribes gave up vast acreages of land for non-Indian settlement in return for separate reservation lands and a multitude of special rights and considerations. Each treaty, although sharing some common characteristics and language with most others, sets forth specific terms governing the relationship between that particular Indian group and the federal government. Consequently, to determine the special rights of a given tribe, its treaty must be carefully examined. Many courts have construed individual treaties. However, perhaps the most important accomplishment of the courts in this area has been their definition of the fundamental nature of Indian treaties.

In 1905, the Supreme Court in *United States v. Winans* issued one of its most important statements about Indian treaties: that Indian rights established in treaties were reservations by the Indians of prior existing rights, and not grants from the federal government. The later *Tee-Hit-Ton Indians v. United States* case emphasized the importance of special Indian treaty rights with its holding that taken rights are not compensable unless they have been recognized by Congress in treaty or statute.

Very early in the history of the United States, the Supreme Court formulated special rules for interpreting Indian treaties. In *Worcester v. Georgia,* the Court held that treaties should never be construed to the prejudice of the Indian signatories. Later decisions emphasized the intent of the parties over technicalities of language, and the understanding of the Indians. *Oliphant v. Suquamish Tribe* provided the most important recent canon of treaty construction by its statement that treaties must be interpreted in light of the times in which they were signed. However, in *Choctaw Nation v. Oklahoma* the Supreme Court limited the interpretive presumption in favor of the Indians by commenting that unfavorable treaties cannot be interpreted so as to rewrite them, even if Indians suffer as a result.

Perhaps the most controversial aspect of Indian treaty interpretation arises when later actions of Congress appear to abrogate treaty provisions. *Menominee Tribe v. United States* asserted the basic requirement that Congress must explicitly state its intent to abrogate a treaty before abrogation should be found. However, this strict standard was later relaxed. As stated in *De Coteau v. District County Court,* courts should determine congressional intent by examining statutory language, legislative history, and the circumstances surrounding the passage of legislation. This broad standard has been applied with increasing frequency in construing Indian rights arising under historic treaties and agreements in light of later statutes.

As more Indian tribes assert special rights based on treaties and agreements, those documents will continue to increase in importance, because they usually are determinative of the rights of the parties to Indian litigation. The Supreme Court's current tendency to search for reasons to justify findings of congressional intent to abrogate Indian treaties creates an unfavorable atmosphere for such assertions of special Indian rights.

1. *Worcester v. Georgia,* 31 U.S. (6 Pet.) 515 (1832).

   (*See* brief at II.A.4)

2. *United States v. Winans,* 198 U.S. 371 (1905).

   (*See* brief at IV.C.2)

3. *United States v. Klamath and Moadoc Tribes of Indians,* 304 U.S. 119 (1938).

Facts: The Tribes lived on a reservation which, by the terms of their treaty, was "to be held until otherwise directed by the President." The government later conveyed 87,000 acres of unallotted reservation land to the California and Oregon Land Company. Although the government paid the Tribes for a release of their claim, it did not include value for standing timber on the land.

Issue: Was the government conveyance of reservation land a taking, entitling the Tribes to just compensation?

Held: (1) Even though the treaty vested in the Tribes only an apparently defeasible interest by the phrase "until otherwise directed by the President," that language "clearly did not detract from the Tribes' right of occupancy."

(2) "[W]hile the United States has power to control and manage the affairs of its Indian wards in good faith for their welfare, that power is subject to constitutional limitations, and does not enable the United States without paying just compensation therefor to appropriate lands of an Indian tribe to its own use or to hand them over to others."

(3) "[T]he timber was a part of the value of the land upon which it was standing. Plaintiffs were entitled to have that element of value included as a part of the compensation for the lands taken."

4. *Choctaw Nation of Indians v. United States,* 318 U.S. 423 (1943).

Facts: The Choctaw and Chickasaw Tribes shared ownership of certain lands which were allotted after the Civil War according to the Treaty of 1866 to freed slaves of the Tribes who the Tribes agreed to adopt. By agreement in 1902, the United States promised to reimburse the Chickasaws for their interests in lands allotted to their freedmen, but the Agreement did not mention the Choctaw freedmen. The Court of Claims construed the Agreement as implying compensation to the Chickasaw Tribe for the Choctaw freedmen allotments.

Issue: Should the 1902 Agreement be construed in favor of the Chickasaw Tribe?

Held: (1) "[T]reaties are construed more liberally than private agreements, and to ascertain their meaning we may look beyond the written words to the history of the treaty, the negotiations, and the practical construction adopted by the parties."

(2) "But even Indian treaties cannot be rewritten or expanded beyond their clear terms to remedy a claimed injustice or to achieve the asserted understanding of the parties."

(3) If the Court implies from the 1902 Agreement that the Chickasaw Tribe is owed compensation, then the Agreement "is rewritten in effect, and this should not be done."

5. *Tee-Hit-Ton Indians v. United States,* 348 U.S. 272 (1955).

Facts: Plaintiffs, a clan of the Tlingit Tribe of Indians, claimed a right of compensation under the Fifth Amendment of the Constitution for the taking of lands to which they formerly held original Indian title, or aboriginal title.

Issue: Was the taking of Tee-Hit-Ton land a compensable Fifth Amendment taking?

Held: (1) Original Indian title "is not a property right but amounts to a right of occupancy which the sovereign grants and protects against intrusion by third parties but which right of occupancy may be terminated and such lands fully disposed of by the sovereign itself without any legally enforceable obligation to compensate the Indians."

(2) To qualify for compensation under the Fifth Amendment, Indian occupancy must be "specifically recognized as ownership by action authorized by Congress."

6. *Menominee Tribe of Indians v. United States,* 391 U.S. 404 (1968).

Facts: The Menominee Tribe claimed they were entitled to compensation for the loss of their hunting and fishing rights allegedly extinguished by the Menominee Termination Act of 1954.

Issue: Did the Tribe have hunting and fishing rights which were extinguished by termination?

Held: (1) Language in the Wolf River Treaty of 1854 creating a reservation, stating that certain lands were set aside "to be held as Indian lands are held," by implication includes hunting and fishing rights on the reservation.

(2) The act terminating federal responsibility over the Menominee Tribe and its property made no mention of hunting and fishing rights. Consequently, "[w]e decline to construe the Termination Act as a backhanded way of abrogating the hunting and fishing rights of these Indians."

(3) "We find it difficult to believe that Congress, without explicit

statement, would subject the United States to a claim for compensation by destroying property rights conferred by treaty. . . ."

7. *Choctaw Nation v. Oklahoma,* 397 U.S. 620 (1970).

Facts: The State of Oklahoma issued oil and gas leases for land underlying the navigable Arkansas River. Several tribes sued for royalties and to stop future interference with their alleged rights to the property. The tribes claimed title to the lands under several treaties with the United States, and the State claimed that title passed to it from the United States upon Oklahoma's becoming a state.

Issue: Did the Indian treaties reserve title to the bed and banks of portions of the Arkansas River for the tribes?

Held: (1) Because treaties were imposed on the Indians, "treaties with the Indians must be interpreted as they would have understood them . . . and any doubtful expressions in them should be resolved in the Indians' favor."

(2) On the basis of the treaty language, which indicates inclusion of the river channel in the reservations, and other circumstances and promises surrounding the treaties, "[w]e thus conclude that the United States intended to and did convey title to the bed of the Arkansas River" to the tribes.

8. *De Coteau v. District County Court,* 420 U.S. 425 (1975).

(*See* brief at IV.B.7)

9. *United States v. Winnebago Tribe of Nebraska,* 542 F.2d 1002 (8th Cir. 1976).

Facts: The United States sought to acquire treaty lands by eminent domain for an Army Corps of Engineers recreational lake.

Issue: Did Congress intend to abrogate the Tribe's treaty rights?

Held: (1) Although Congress has the power to abrogate treaty rights, there must be "a clear expression of congressional purpose."

(2) Here, there was no reference in the legislative history of the proposed taking of Indian trust lands for the project. Thus, "[t]he United States . . . was without authority to take the Tribal lands at issue by eminent domain."

10. *Rosebud Sioux Tribe v. Kneip,* 430 U.S. 585 (1977).

Facts: The Rosebud Sioux Tribe sought a declaratory judgment that congressional acts in the early 1900s opening their reservation to non-Indian settlement did not diminish the reservation.

Issue: Were the reservation boundaries diminished by these acts of Congress?

Held: (1) The general rule interpreting treaties and statutes is that "doubtful expressions" should be interpreted in favor of Indians, and "[t]he mere fact that a reservation has been opened to settlement does not necessarily mean that the opened area has lost its reservation status." However, "the 'general rule' does not command a determination that reservation status survives in the face of congressionally manifested intent to the contrary."

(2) Language of the act, its legislative history, and "surrounding circumstances" should be examined to determine congressional intent.

(3) Language of the cession agreements that the Indians "cede, surrender, grant, and convey to the United States all their claim, right, title, and interest" in the disputed areas, taken in light of the circumstances of the acts, indicate that Congress intended to diminish the reservation.

11. *Oliphant v. Suquamish Indian Tribe,* 435 U.S. 191 (1978).
(*See* brief at III.B.5)

12. *United States v. Dion,* 476 U.S. 734 (1986).
(*See* brief at IV.C.14)

B. Indian Lands

When the federal government first restricted Indian tribes to reservations, either through treaties, agreements, or executive orders, few questions arose regarding the nature of the Indian landholding. Usually reservations were isolated from non-Indian communities, and land disputes occurred only when an encroaching white society saw potential economic uses for Indian land or its products.

United States v. Shoshone Tribe, in 1938, specifically addressed a federal taking of only part of a reservation. However, it was a landmark in its determination of the nature of Indian reservation occupancy. The Supreme Court characterized Indian beneficial title "as sacred as the fee," which included ownership of all attached minerals and natural resources. Much later, in *United States v. Jim,* the Court further defined reservation ownership as vested in the Indian tribe, not Indian individuals. However, that decision also confirmed the plenary power of Congress to administer tribal property according to its view of the Indians' best interests.

One common dispute over Indian reservation land has been whether Indian tribes own the beds and banks of navigable waterways flowing through their reservations. In *United States v. Holt State Bank,* the Supreme Court in 1926 asserted the presumption of state ownership, and set out the factors to be examined before that presumption can be overcome and tribal ownership found: the language of the treaty, and the finding of a public exigency in favor of the tribe owning the beds and banks. This issue, with ramifications for jurisdiction, hunting and fishing, and perhaps even water rights, has been a subject for dispute ever since. Federal courts have decided ownership on a case-by-case basis, sometimes finding tribal ownership, as in *Choctaw Nation v. Oklahoma* and *Confederated Salish and Kootenai Tribes v. Namen,* and other times finding state ownership, as in *Montana v. United States.* This tedious approach will, no doubt, continue.

Another aspect of Indian tribal landholding was considered during the 1940s and 1950s as tribes asserted compensation claims against the United States for alleged takings of their land. In 1942, the Supreme Court in *Sioux Tribe v. United States* held that although the President has the authority to create reservations by executive order, tribes are not entitled to compensation for the taking of those reservation lands without additional express congressional authorization. The Court reached a similar conclusion later in *Tee-Hit-Ton Indians v. United States,* requiring congressional recognition of Indian ownership before the Indians are entitled to compensation under the Fifth Amendment for the taking of aboriginal lands.

In the early part of the twentieth century, cases addressing Indian lands issues established some basic rules about their nature and treatment. However, federal courts continue to be confronted by demands for specific applications of those rules in disputes among the tribes, the states, and the federal government. As long as conflicts among those parties over Indian lands persist, this litigious pattern likely will continue.

1. *United States v. Holt State Bank,* 270 U.S. 49 (1926).

Facts: Mud Lake was within the former Red Lake Chippewa Reservation. After the Indians ceded the reservation to the United States, the Lake was drained and the United States prepared to dispose of the lake bed for the benefit of the Indians. The government filed suit to quiet title to the lake bed.

Issue: Did the United States own the lake bed?

Held: (1) A long-standing policy of the United States is that lands under navigable waters which are acquired by the government are held in trust for future states. Title to these lands passes to the state "save in exceptional instances when impelled to particular disposals by some international duty or public exigency."

(2) Streams and lakes are navigable if "the stream in its natural and ordinary condition affords a channel for useful commerce," without regard to the type of vessels or "occasional difficulties of navigation." Mud Lake was a navigable water.

(3) The Red Lake Reservation was not formally set aside for the Indians, and no effort was made to restrict use of its navigable waters. "There was nothing . . . which even approaches a grant of rights in lands underlying navigable waters; nor anything evincing a purpose to depart from the established policy . . . of treating such lands as held for the benefit of the future State."

2. *United States v. Shoshone Tribe of Indians,* 304 U.S. 111 (1938).

Facts: The United States placed an Arapahoe band on the Shoshone Reservation, in violation of the treaty with the Shoshone. It was established that the government owed compensation to the Shoshones for this taking of their land, but the government objected to compensating the Tribe for timber and minerals.

Issue: Did the Tribe's "right of occupancy" include timber and mineral resources?

Held: (1) "The right of occupancy [is] as sacred as the fee"; the United States could not give away or appropriate the lands without just compensation to the Tribe--"that would be, not the exercise of guardianship or management, but confiscation."

(2) "Minerals and standing timber are constituent elements of the land itself. For all practical purposes, the tribe owned the land" (especially when the treaties are interpreted "in the sense in which naturally the Indians would have understood them").

3. *Sioux Tribe v. United States,* 316 U.S. 317 (1942).

Facts: Certain tracts of land were set aside for the Tribe by executive order, in order to help control the liquor trade. A few years later, subsequent executive orders returned these lands to the public domain.

Issue: Did the President have the power to bestow on the Tribe a compensable interest in an executive order reservation?

Held: (1) "Where lands have been received for. . . an Indian Tribe by. . . treaty or statute, the tribe must be compensated if the lands are subsequently taken from them."

(2) But although Congress has acquiesced in the President's power to withdraw lands from the public domain (despite Article IV, Section 3 of the Constitution which places such power exclusively with Congress), "there was no express constitutional or statutory authorization for the conveyance of a compensable interest" by this method.

(3) The Tribe is not entitled to compensation for the taking.

4. *Tee-Hit-Ton Indians v. United States,* 348 U.S. 272 (1955).

(*See* brief at IV.A.5)

5. *Choctaw Nation v. Oklahoma,* 397 U.S. 620 (1970).

(*See* brief at IV.A.7)

6. *United States v. Jim,* 409 U.S. 80 (1972).

Facts: In 1933, Congress added land to the Navajo Reservation, with the requirement that royalties from mineral resources on the land be used "for the benefit of the Indians residing therein." In 1968, Congress directed that the royalties be used for the benefit of Navajos "residing in San Juan County," a larger area, thus diminishing the share of the residents of the original area.

Issue: Was this expansion of the mineral benefits to a large area a "taking" from the residents of the original, smaller area?

Held: (1) The title to the added land was "in the tribe, and not in the individuals, although held by the tribe for the common use and equal benefit of all the members."

(2) Congress has "administrative control . . . over the tribal property of tribal Indians," and thus could alter the distributional scheme. There was no "taking" from the residents because there was no "property" held by them.

7. *De Coteau v. District County Court,* 420 U.S. 425 (1975).

Facts: An 1889 agreement between the Tribe and the United States, adopted by an 1891 Act, sold "all the unallotted land within the limits of the reservation." This resulted in 85 percent of the reservation being opened to non-Indian settlement. The resident population in 1975 was 3,000 Indian and 30,000 non-Indian. The Court looked to newspaper accounts in determining congressional intent.

Issue: Did the "face of the Act" or the "surrounding circumstances and legislative history" make clear Congress' intent to disestablish the reservation?

Held: (1) "A canon of construction [benefiting Indians] is not a license to disregard clear expressions of tribal and congressional intent."

(2) The facts of this case indicate that the Indians were willing to cede all their interest in tribal lands, "point[ing] unmistakably to the conclusion that the . . . reservation was terminated in 1891."

8. *United States v. Southern Pacific Transportation Co.,* 543 F.2d 676 (9th Cir. 1976).

Facts: The Tribe alleged that a railway which passed through its reservation (an executive order reservation) was a trespasser. The railway claimed that it had a valid right-of-way due to (1) conveyance of an easement by the Tribe; (2) a subsequent act of Congress granting railway rights-of-way through reservations; (3) subsequent disestablishment of the reservation; or (4) license from the Tribe.

Issue: Did the railway have a valid right-of-way?

Held: (1) The Railroad Right-of-Way Act of 1875 excepted Indian reservations; this included "executive order" reservations, as well as those created by treaty or statute.

(2) Mere approval by the Secretary of the Interior of the railway's maps did not "terminate the reservation."

(3) An 1899 Railroad Right-of-Way Act did not retroactively approve the railway's trespass.

(4) A "license" does not arise when an easement fails under the Indian Nonintercourse Act.

(5) But a 1906 "cession did change the reservation boundary, and the railway's right-of-way was valid over the ceded lands from 1906 onwards."

9. *Northern Cheyenne Tribe v. Hollowbreast,* 425 U.S. 649 (1976).

Facts: The Northern Cheyenne Allotment Act provided that mineral rights in allotments were "reserved for the benefit of the tribe" for fifty years, and that Congress retained control and management of the "unallotted lands." Congress later terminated the grant of mineral rights to the allottees and reserved those rights "in perpetuity for the benefit of the Tribe."

Issue: Were the mineral rights a "vested future interest" of the allottees, so that Congress' "taking" was compensable?

Held: (1) The statutory history shows a clear intention to reserve the mineral interests for the entire Tribe, and grant "agricultural lands" to allottees.

(2) Allotment statutes "are to be read to reserve Congress' powers in the absence of a clear expression . . . to the contrary."

(3) Thus, "unallotted lands" over which Congress retained control and management included the mineral deposits.

10. *Wilson v. Omaha Indian Tribe,* 442 U.S. 653 (1979).

Facts: The Missouri River changed its course, so that a large peninsula on the west side now joined the east side. The Omaha Tribe and the State of Iowa disputed ownership.

Issue: Was this land covered by the Omahas' 1854 treaty, or did the change in course from 1927 on mean that it was part of Iowa?

Held: (1) Federal law applies, because the case arises under the 1854 treaty.

(2) Section 194 of 25 U.S.C., a part of the Trade and Intercourse Acts which placed the burden of proof in land disputes on the non-Indian party, applies to tribal lands and against corporations as well as against white individuals. But, it does not apply against state litigants.

(3) Federal law should adopt state law in determining whether river changes are avulsive or accretive.

11. *Montana v. United States,* 450 U.S. 544 (1981).

(*See* brief at IV.C.10)

12. *Confederated Salish and Kootenai Tribes v. Namen,* 665 F.2d 951 (9th Cir. 1982), *cert. denied,* 459 U.S. 977 (1982).

(*See* brief at III.A.2.10)

C. Hunting and Fishing Rights

One underlying purpose of Indian treaties was to enable the Indians to sustain themselves so as to maintain their livelihood on the reservations. Some treaties expressly guaranteed that Indians could continue certain subsistence activities (including hunting and fishing primarily, but also gathering, cutting timber, and grazing livestock) *outside* the boundaries of their reservations, in common with non-Indian citizens. All treaties expressly or impliedly reserved an exclusive right for tribes to carry out subsistence activities *inside* their reservations. These guarantees are generally known as "reserved rights." Courts have spent almost a century grappling with these subsistence rights themselves, governmental jurisdiction over such rights, and Congress' intentions towards them.

The first issues dealt with by the courts involved off-reservation reserved rights. Exercise of these rights often carried Indians great distances from their reservations. As non-Indian settlement increased in and around Indian territories, conflicts arose first over the "in common" exploitation of resources outside of reservations. Only later, when many reservations were opened to non-Indian settlement pursuant to allotment acts and other congressional enactments, did on-reservation conflicts arise.

Near the turn of the century, the Supreme Court determined the nature of most off-reservation treaty reserved rights. *Ward v. Race Horse* held that some rights were implicitly defeasible. By the terms of the treaty, as they were understood by the treaty signatories, these particular off-reservation reserved rights were expected to contract commensurate with the expansion of non-Indian settlement on open lands. The other major holding of this case, that Indian treaty rights terminate when a territory becomes a state through the Equal Footing Doctrine, has been silently overruled by many later Supreme Court decisions.

A few years after *Race Horse,* in *United States v. Winans,* the Supreme Court found that off-reservation treaty rights were property rights--servitudes on the land--which survived despite changes in land ownership. Much later, tribal reserved rights were held to be communal rights of the tribe, for which only the tribe, not individual Indians, was entitled to compensation for their taking.

In the late 1960s, the Supreme Court in *Menominee Tribe v. United States* found that exclusive on-reservation hunting and fishing rights could be inferred from the nature of Indian occupancy, even in the absence of express treaty language. In addition, when confronted with the prospect of compensating the Menominee Tribe for those rights after the Tribe's termination, the Court held that their hunting and fishing rights survived termination, in the absence of explicit congressional language to the contrary.

Disputes with states over the regulation of off-reservation hunting and fishing rights arose as game resources became scarce. *Puyallup Tribe v. Department of Game (Puyallup I)* devastated state aspirations with its holding that states could not regulate off-reservation treaty fishing rights, except through non-discriminatory regulation directed toward conservation of the species, with the burden of proof on the state. Jurisdiction again was the basis for the *State v. Tinno* case, in which anthropological and linguistic evidence supported the Idaho Supreme Court's conclusion that treaty language reserving off-reservation hunting rights also reserved fishing rights. This era of treaty language and jurisdictional disputes culminated with *United States v. Washington.* It confirmed the general lack of state jurisdiction over Indian off-reservation treaty fishing rights and defined the Indian "in-common" share of fish as up to fifty percent of the harvest. *Washington v. Washington State Commercial Passenger Fishing Vessel Association* confirmed that the 50 percent allocation was a maximum amount, and that Indian treaty rights grant rights only to the amount of a natural resource that is necessary to provide a moderate living, and no more.

In the past few years, Indian hunting and fishing rights have had a mixed reception in the courts. Although *Montana v. United States* seemed to eliminate tribal jurisdiction over non-Indian hunting and fishing on non-Indian land even when the land was within reservation boundaries, the *New Mexico v. Mescalero* case strongly asserted tribal sovereignty over on-reservation regulation of hunting and fishing on a reservation without any non-Indian land within its boundaries. In addition, the court in *Blake v. Arnett* found that on-reservation tribal rights did not encumber Indian allotments or former allotments now in fee ownership.

The Supreme Court in *United States v. Dion* extended its relatively recent doctrine of not requiring explicit statutory abrogation language by holding that the Eagle Protection Act abrogated the Indian on-reservation right to hunt eagles. Finally, *United States v. Eberhardt* explicitly confirmed that the Secretary of the Interior, under his general statutory power to manage Indian affairs, can regulate Indian hunting and fishing himself, without additional congressional authority. This power has been confirmed more recently in *Northern Arapahoe Tribe v. Hodel.* All of these recent cases make it difficult to predict accurately the future attitudes of the judiciary toward Indian hunting and fishing rights.

1. *Ward v. Race Horse,* 163 U.S. 504 (1896).

Facts: The Fort Bridger Treaty of 1868 reserved "the right to hunt upon the unoccupied lands of the United States . . . so long as peace subsists among the whites and Indians on the borders of the hunting districts." A tribal member killed an elk outside the reservation in violation of Wyoming state game regulations.

Issue: Did the Tribe have a treaty right to hunt free of Wyoming state regulation?

Held: (1) "Unoccupied lands of the United States," where the right to hunt was reserved, are lands owned by the United States contained within traditional hunting districts.

(2) "The right to hunt given by the treaty clearly contemplated the disappearance of the condition therein specified," since "the right depended on whether the land . . . was unoccupied public lands of the United States." In fact, "the right to hunt should cease the moment the United States parted with the title to its land in the hunting districts. No restraint was imposed by the treaty on the power of the United States to sell" its land.

(3) Wyoming was admitted to the Union on an equal footing with the original States, and the continued existence of the treaty right to hunt would deprive the State "of a legislative power [of regulating the killing of game] vested in all the other States." The treaty right is repealed by action of "the conflict between the treaty and the [later] act admitting that State into the Union."

2. *United States v. Winans,* 198 U.S. 371 (1905).

Facts: The Yakima Treaty reserved the right to fish "at all usual and accustomed places, in common with citizens of the Territory." The United States sought an injunction against private landowners to keep them from obstructing Yakima Indians from exercising their treaty fishing rights on the Columbia River.

Issue: Can private landowners keep tribal members from exercising their treaty fishing rights?

Held: (1) "[T]he treaty was not a grant of rights to the Indians, but a grant of rights from them--a reservation of those not granted."

(2) The fishing right is a servitude on the land. "The contingency of the future ownership of the land, therefore, was foreseen and provided for--in other words, the Indians were given a right in the land--the right of crossing it to the river--the right to occupy it to the extent and for the purpose mentioned."

3. *Whitefoot v. United States,* 155 Ct. Cl. 127 (1961), *cert. denied,* 369 U.S. 818 (1962).

Facts: The Treaty with the Yakima Tribe guaranteed a compensable right to fish at usual and accustomed places. In 1950, Congress enacted legislation for construction of the Dalles Dam on the Columbia River, which would inundate numerous of these fishing places. By agreement with the United States, the Yakima Tribe was paid $15 million in compensation for the loss of its fishing rights. Plaintiff tribal members claim individual ownership of several fishing places, and assert that the per-capita distribution of compensation funds was inadequate. They sued the government for compensation for the taking of their individual property.

Issue: Are these individual tribal members entitled to compensation for the taking of a fishing place?

Held: (1) The Yakima Tribe communally held the right to fish as guaranteed in their treaty, "in accord with normal Indian custom." The Tribe received payment for its rights.

(2) "[T]he use of accustomed fishing places, whether on or off the reservation, is a tribal right for adjustment by the tribe and . . . the fact that certain Indians have been allowed to have sole use of a particular spot by the Tribe gives that individual no property right against the Tribe. . . ."

4. *Organized Village of Kake v. Egan,* 369 U.S. 60 (1962).

Facts: The Secretary of the Interior issued regulations permitting non-reservation Indians to operate fish traps in Alaska. The State arrested the Indians for violating its anti-fish-trap laws.

Issue: Did the Secretary's regulations override state laws?

Held: (1) "Even on reservations state laws may be applied to Indians unless such application would interfere with reservation self-government or impair a right granted or reserved by federal law."

(2) "State authority over Indians is yet more extensive over activities . . . not on any reservation."

(3) Since Congress had not empowered the Secretary to authorize the fish traps, the state law was valid.

5. *Puyallup Tribe v. Department of Game (Puyallup I),* 391 U.S. 392 (1968).

Facts: The Treaty of Medicine Creek provided that "the right of taking fish, at all usual and accustomed grounds and stations, is further secured to said Indians, in common with all citizens of the Territory."

The Indians used "set nets" for commercial and subsistence fishing, contrary to state law.

Issue: Did state law apply to tribal off-reservation fishing?

Held: (1) The "Treaty is silent as to the mode or modes of fishing that are guaranteed." Thus, "the manner of fishing, the size of the take, the restriction of commercial fishing, and the like may be regulated by the State in the interest of conservation, provided the regulation meets appropriate standards and does not discriminate against the Indians."

(2) The treaty fishing right, even with its commercial aspects, cannot "be qualified by the State, even though all Indians born in the United States are now citizens of the United States."

(3) The ban on "set nets" is not discriminatory, because it applies "not only to Indians but to all others."

(4) Whether the ban on set nets is a "reasonable and necessary conservation measure" was remanded for determination.

6. *Menominee Tribe of Indians v. United States,* 391 U.S. 404 (1968).

(*See* brief at IV.A.6)

7. *State v. Tinno,* 94 Idaho 759, 497 P.2d 1386 (1972).

Facts: Defendant was charged with spear-fishing in violation of state regulation.

Issue: Did a treaty right protecting off-reservation "hunting" also protect fishing rights?

Held: Under the Indian language, "hunt" included "to fish." Thus, interpreting the treaty the way the Indians would have understood it, defendant had the right to fish free of state regulation.

8. *United States v. Washington,* 520 F.2d 676 (9th Cir. 1975), *cert. denied,* 423 U.S. 1086 (1976).

Facts: The United States brought suit as trustee for a number of western Washington Indian tribes against the State of Washington regarding the Indians' exercise of their off-reservation treaty fishing rights.

Issue: What is the nature of the Indian treaty fishing rights, and what are the regulatory roles of the State and the tribes?

Held: (1) These Indians, with the right to fish "in common with citizens of the Territory," should have the opportunity to take up to 50 percent of the harvestable catch of fish.

(2) Fish caught on the reservation, where tribal members have an exclusive right to fish, will be excluded from the 50 percent apportionment.

(3) "[T]he state . . . can regulate off-reservation fishing by treaty Indians at their usual and accustomed grounds only if . . . the regulation is reasonable and necessary for conservation . . . the perpetuation of a run or of a species of fish."

(4) "Those treaty tribes meeting certain qualifying requirements . . . may regulate fishing by their own members free from any state regulation."

9. *Washington v. Washington State Commercial Passenger Fishing Vessel Association,* 443 U.S. 658 (1979).

Facts: Involved Indian treaties guaranteed the Indians the "right of taking fish, at usual and accustomed grounds and stations . . . in common with all citizens of the Territory." The state and federal courts conflicted in interpreting this language.

Issue: To what extent did this treaty language guarantee tribal off-reservation fishing rights to harvest anadromous fish?

Held: (1) The special benefits conferred on Indians under the treaty do not violate the Equal Protection Clause of the Fourteenth Amendment.

(2) The treaty's words must be construed "in the sense in which they would naturally be understood by Indians."

(3) The words "in common with" and "right of *taking* fish" suggest an entitlement to a share of fish, rather than just an equal opportunity to fish.

(4) Like hunting rights and water rights, Indian fishing rights are reserved by the tribe, not granted to the tribe. The Indians are entitled to a *maximum* of 50 percent of the harvestable portion of each run, but just as with treaty rights to any natural resource, "not more than is necessary to provide the Indians with a livelihood--that is to say, a moderate living."

(5) The federal courts have the power to enforce their orders even to the extent of displacing "local enforcement of those orders if necessary to remedy the violations of federal law found by the court."

10. *Montana v. United States,* 450 U.S. 544 (1981).

Facts: The Crow Tribe claimed the authority to prohibit or regulate hunting and fishing by non-members of the Tribe on the reservation, including on non-Indian property within the reservation.

Issue: Did the Tribe have title to the bed of the Big Horn River which flowed through the reservation? Could the Tribe prohibit or regulate non-member fishing and hunting on non-Indian lands within the reservation?

Held: (1) The United States retained title to the river bed when the reservation was established, and that title passed to Montana upon entering the Union, under the "equal footing" doctrine. This rule applies to navigable waters, particularly where fishing was not important to the Tribe's way of life and where the treaty lands were not within the Tribe's aboriginal territory.

(2) The allotment of Crow lands reduced the amount of land "set apart for the absolute and undisturbed use and occupancy" of the Tribe. The Tribe's power to restrict non-Indian hunting and fishing applied only to such lands.

(3) The Tribe does not have "inherent sovereignty" to restrict non-Indian hunting and fishing on non-Indian lands on the reservation. Such authority would be inconsistent with the Tribe's status as a domestic dependent nation. Inherent sovereignty only extends to "tribal self-government and internal relations."

(4) A tribe may exercise "some forms of civil jurisdiction over non-Indians on their reservations, even on non-Indian fee lands," particularly when non-members have entered "consensual relationships" with the tribe or when their conduct "threatens the Tribe's political or economic security," or the "health or welfare of the tribe."

(5) However, "nothing in this case suggests that such non-Indian hunting and fishing so threatens the Tribe's political or economic security as to justify tribal regulation."

11. *Blake v. Arnett,* 663 F.2d 906 (9th Cir. 1981).

Facts: Simpson Timber Company owned land within the old Klamath River Indian Reservation, as non-Indian successor to individual Indian allottees and non-Indians who received patents when the reservation was opened to non-Indian settlement. Yurok tribal members claimed the right to enter and cross Simpson's land to exercise their tribal hunting and fishing rights.

Issue: Are tribal on-reservation hunting and fishing rights exercisable on former allotments and patented lands within the boundaries of the reservation?

Held: (1) The Executive Order creating the reservation impliedly reserved the tribal rights to hunt and fish within the reservation.

(2) If tribal rights exist on Simpson's land, they must be "a form of equitable servitude that benefits the tribe and burdens the land,

whoever owns it." However, "[w]e conclude that Congress intended that the allotments and patents, granted under the Act of 1887, would grant an unencumbered title to the Indian allottees and their successors in interest, which would not be subject to any interest in the land that might be implied from the mere creation of the reservation." Thus, Yurok tribal members cannot exercise their tribal hunting and fishing rights on Simpson's land.

12. *New Mexico v. Mescalero Apache Tribe,* 462 U.S. 333 (1983).

Facts: Non-Indians were arrested by state authorities for hunting on the reservation without complying with state regulations. The hunters were in compliance with the Tribe's comprehensive fish and game management program. The federal government was extensively involved in the tribal fish and wildlife operations. Almost all the reservation land was tribally owned.

Issue: Was state regulation of on-reservation hunting preempted?

Held: (1) Unlike *Montana,* this case concerns lands belonging to the Tribe. In addition, the State cannot point to off-reservation effects that necessitate state intervention in the interests of conservation, and the hunting and fishing activity involved here concerns value generated on the reservation by the Tribe.

(2) "The tribe's authority to regulate hunting and fishing," approved by the Secretary of the Interior and implemented with strong federal support, "preempts state jurisdiction." "State jurisdiction is preempted by the operation of federal law if it interferes or is incompatible with federal and tribal interests reflected in federal law, unless the state interests at stake are sufficient to justify the assertion of state authority." Here, the only state interest was a "general desire to obtain revenues." That is not enough to justify jurisdiction.

13. *Oregon Department of Fish and Wildlife v. Klamath Indian Tribe,* 473 U.S. 753 (1985).

Facts: The Klamath Treaty of 1864 reserved the right to hunt, fish, and trap within the Klamath Reservation, with no rights reserved outside its boundaries. In 1901, an agreement was ratified by Congress whereby the Tribe agreed to cede "all their claim, right, title, and interest in and to" a portion of the Reservation. The Tribe sought an injunction against the State of Oregon to end interference with tribal members' hunting and fishing on these ceded lands.

Issue: Does the Tribe retain the right to hunt and fish free of state regulation on this ceded portion of the 1864 reservation?

Held: (1) The treaty reserved exclusive rights to hunt and fish on the reservation. However, "[t]he fact that the rights were characterized as 'exclusive' forecloses the possibility that they were intended to have existence outside of the reservation; no exclusivity would be possible on lands open to non-Indians."

(2) No compensation for the ceded land was specifically earmarked for hunting and fishing rights. However, "the fact that there was no separate valuation . . . is consistent with the view that the parties did not understand any such separate right to exist, and that the value of fish, game, and vegetation on the ceded lands was subsumed within the estimated value of the land in general."

(3) "The broad language used in the 1901 Agreement . . . accomplished a diminution of the reservation . . . and no language . . . evidences any intent to preserve special off-reservation hunting or fishing rights for the Tribe."

14. *United States v. Dion,* 476 U.S. 734 (1986).

Facts: An Indian defendant killed several bald eagles on the Yankton Sioux Reservation. He was convicted of a violation of the Endangered Species Act, and the district court dismissed a charge against him under the Eagle Protection Act. Defendant claimed the Yankton Sioux Treaty of 1858 reserved for the Tribe the exclusive right to hunt on reservation lands, including hunting eagles.

Issue: Do the Endangered Species Act and the Eagle Protection Act abrogate Sioux treaty rights to hunt eagles?

Held: (1) The Court requires that Congress must reveal, through statutory language or other evidence, its intention to abrogate Indian treaty rights. "What is essential is clear evidence that Congress actually considered the conflict between its intended action on the one hand and Indian treaty rights on the other, and chose to resolve that conflict by abrogating the treaty."

(2) The inclusion of a provision in the Eagle Protection Act allowing Indian tribes to take eagles for religious purposes under a permit, taken with the rest of the Act's legislative history, clearly indicates "that Congress in 1962 believed that it was abrogating the rights of Indians to take eagles."

(3) "[W]e need not resolve the question of whether the Congress in the Endangered Species Act abrogated Indian treaty rights." Since by passage and amendment of the Eagle Protection Act, Congress "divested Dion of his treaty right to hunt bald eagles . . . [h]e therefore has no treaty right to hunt bald eagles that he can assert as a defense to an Endangered Species Act charge."

15. *United States v. Eberhardt,* 789 F.2d 1354 (9th Cir. 1986).

Facts: Tribal members were arrested and charged with violation of Department of the Interior regulations prohibiting commercial fishing for anadromous fish on the Hoopa Valley Reservation. The district court dismissed the charges, holding the regulations to be an invalid modification or abrogation of the Indians' treaty right to fish commercially.

Issue: Was the Department of the Interior authorized to prohibit commercial fishing on the reservation?

Held: (1) "[T]he general trust statutes in Title 25 [§§ 2 and 9] do furnish Interior with broad authority to supervise and manage Indian affairs and property commensurate with the trust obligations of the United States." Thus, Interior was authorized to issue these fishing regulations.

(2) "Interior's regulations are designed to manage the fishery for the benefit of the Indians, not to extinguish any reserved tribal fishing rights." Because Interior has broader authority than do states to regulate Indian fishing, Interior is not required "to justify the ban on commercial fishing by showing that the fish resources . . . were facing imminent extinction."

(3) Because no evidence was introduced showing improper rule-making procedures, "there is no basis to invalidate these regulations despite their impact in managing the fishing rights of Hoopa Valley Reservation Indians."

16. *Northern Arapahoe Tribe v. Hodel,* 808 F.2d 741 (10th Cir. 1987).

Facts: Both the Northern Arapahoe and Shoshone Tribes reside on the Wind River Indian Reservation in Wyoming. Although the Tribes agreed that wildlife was becoming more scarce on the reservation because of a lack of management, they could not agree on a common regulatory scheme. Finally, the Shoshone Tribe requested that the Bureau of Indian Affairs enact federal regulations. The Bureau adopted interim wildlife management regulations, effective immediately, under the "good cause" provision of the Administrative Procedure Act. The Northern Arapahoe Tribe sued for declaratory and injunctive relief from the regulations.

Issue: Does the Secretary of the Interior, through the Bureau of Indian Affairs, have the authority to regulate tribal hunting and fishing on the reservation?

Held: (1) The Shoshone possess implied hunting and fishing rights on the reservation under the treaty which set aside the reservation for their "absolute and undisturbed use and occupation." Also, "[t]he

Arapahoe have rights to the reservation derived from their status as occupants of the land confirmed by congressional and executive acts." Thus, "the Shoshone and the Arapahoe have equal rights to hunt on the reservation."

(2) "The right to hunt on the reservation is held in common by both tribes, and one tribe cannot claim that right to a point of endangering the resource in derogation of the other tribe's rights."

(3) The Shoshone treaty "was intended to preserve for the Shoshone a reservation land base with sufficient resources to supply the needs of the Indian people who settled thereon." Considering the treaty and the general trust relationship between the United States and Indian tribes, "the Government has the right upon request of the Shoshone to protect the resources guaranteed the Shoshone by treaty from misappropriation by third parties."

(4) In light of the potential harm of unregulated hunting to reservation wildlife, "there were sufficient indicia of urgency to warrant the imposition of the regulations on an interim basis," particularly considering the Arapahoe had been consulted and were aware that federal regulation was imminent.

D. Water Rights

Water rights issues have been hotly litigated for over a century, primarily because of the need for water in the arid American West for any kind of development. Indian water rights became the subject of much litigation because of the vast acreages set aside for Indian reservations, and the sometimes enormous quantities of water which the Indians claim are necessary for them to survive there. As early as 1908, Indians fought against the diversion of water from their lands. In *Winters v. United States,* the Supreme Court laid the foundation for Indian water rights by finding an implied congressional reservation of water sufficient to fulfill the purposes of Indian reservations established by treaty. Most all Indian water rights cases since that time have been attempts to define further the Indian "*Winters* Rights."

After the General Allotment Act and the expiration of the initial 25-year trust period, the alienation of allotments into fee ownership first raised questions about the non-Indian successors' water rights. The landmark *United States v. Hibner* decision found treaty-reserved water rights arising from irrigation, as the primary purpose of the reservation. The priority date for those rights, both on tribal and allotment lands, would be the date of establishment of the reservation. When allotments passed into fee ownership, the non-Indian successors acquired water rights based on the actual acreage under irrigation at the date of transfer, plus that which could be irrigated with reasonable diligence, all with the allottees' priority date of reservation establishment. The Supreme Court in *United States v. Powers* later confirmed this basic policy.

The first *Arizona v. California* case defined specific issues for later litigation. The Supreme Court held that Indian water rights were intended for both present and future needs, and that quantification of those rights should be based on the practicably irrigable acreage on the reservations. As more adjudications began in the 1970s, the *Colorado River Water Conservation District v. United States* case definitively stated that the McCarran Amendment waived United States sovereign immunity in water rights adjudications, and encouraged federal courts, which have concurrent jurisdiction with state courts, to defer to state court proceedings.

Recent cases reflect tribal concerns over water adjudications in state courts and the movement toward more specific definitions of the extent of Indian water rights. *Colville Confederated Tribes v. Walton* broadly interpreted reservation purposes to include maintenance of a fishery, and found a reserved water right to support it. This court also went farther than any other in holding that tribes may put their water to any lawful use, allottees may sell their water, and states cannot regulate any Indian reservation water. However, that same court later found that states may regulate excess water on reservations that have been opened to non-Indian settlement. Hunting and fishing issues were addressed in *United States v. Adair,* in which the court based water rights quantification on current necessity to maintain the livelihood of tribal members.

The Supreme Court recently has addressed more basic issues. It held that the United States can represent both tribal interests and conflicting governmental interests concurrently during water adjudications, and confirmed the desirability of state court jurisdiction. In addition, the Court upheld the practically irrigable acreage standard in affirming (by an equally divided court) the Wyoming adjudication of water rights in the Big Horn River system. More lawsuits will no doubt follow these, as Indian tribes attempt to retain their implied water rights in the face of potentially hostile adverse interests and potentially conflicting federal advocacy.

1. *Winters v. United States,* 207 U.S. 564 (1908).

Facts: The Tribe ceded part of its reservation, and the ceded lands were opened to white settlers. The settlers diverted water from the Milk River for agricultural irrigation, thereby preventing sufficient water for the Indians' use from reaching the Indian lands.

Issue: Does the State's prior appropriation doctrine mean that the white settlers' prior appropriation of water for a beneficial use prevails over Indian use?

Held: (1) The reservation was established to help the Indians become "a pastoral and civilized people," but without irrigation the reservation lands "were practically valueless."

(2) "The Indians had command of the land and waters . . . whether kept for hunting . . . or turned to agriculture and the arts of civilization" and cannot be presumed to have given up all the water which made their land valuable.

(3) The government reserved the waters for the Indians and exempted them from state prior appropriation laws, "for a use which would be necessarily continued through years."

2. *United States v. Hibner,* 27 F.2d 909 (D. Idaho 1928).

Facts: The United States sought adjudication of the water rights of Indian allottees and their non-Indian successors for the use of Toponce Creek. The land involved was formerly within the Fort Hall Reservation.

Issue: What are the water rights of Indian allottees and their non-Indian successors?

Held: (1) "[T]he effect of the treaties was to recognize and fix permanently the rights that the Indians had at the time the treaties were made, which was to a continuous use of a sufficient amount of water for the irrigation of their lands, and domestic purposes." This right attaches to lands "susceptible to irrigation," and carries a priority date of the ratification of the treaty.

(2) "[T]he failure of the Indians to use their water will not cause either an abandonment or a forfeiture of their rights thereto."

(3) The non-Indian successor fee owner of an Indian allotment would "be entitled to a water right for the actual acreage that was under irrigation at the time title passed from the Indians, and such increased acreage as he might with reasonable diligence place under irrigation," with "the same priority as owned by the Indians."

3. *United States v. Powers,* 305 U.S. 527 (1939).

Facts: Non-Indian fee owners of former Indian allotments within the reservation diverted water for irrigation from non-navigable streams within the reservation. The United States filed for an injunction against any further use or diversion of the water, asserting the control of the Secretary of the Interior over reservation waters.

Issue: What water rights are retained by non-Indian fee owners of former reservation allotments?

Held: (1) "[U]nder the Treaty of 1868 waters within the Reservation were reserved for the equal benefit of tribal members and . . . when allotments of land were duly made for exclusive use and thereafter conveyed in fee, the right to use some portion of tribal waters essential for cultivation passed to the owners."

(2) The Allotment Act "indicates Congressional recognition of equal rights among resident Indians." Although the Secretary was authorized to regulate distribution of reservation waters, "he could not affirmatively authorize unjust and unequal distribution."

4. *Arizona v. California (I),* 373 U.S. 546 (1963).

Facts: Indian tribes and the State differed over the amount of water from the Colorado River to which the tribes were entitled. Some of the reservation lands were added by executive order.

Issue: Do water rights under the *Winters* doctrine extend to executive order reservations? What is the amount of water reserved under the *Winters* doctrine?

Held: (1) "An Indian Reservation is not a State." Thus, the doctrine of equitable apportionment for resolving interstate water disputes does not apply.

(2) The federal government has the power, under the Commerce Clause and Article IV, Section 3 of the Constitution, "to reserve water rights for its reservations."

(3) Reservations created by executive order include water rights.

(4) Indian water rights were created "as of the time the Indian Reservations were created." They are "entitled to priority" as "present perfected rights."

(5) "The water was intended to satisfy the future as well as the present needs of the Indian Reservations and . . . enough water was reserved to irrigate all the practicably irrigable acreage on the reservations."

5. *Colorado River Water Conservation District v. United States,* 424 U.S. 800 (1976).

Facts: The federal government brought suit in federal court for a declaration of water rights, including Indian water rights, in certain rivers. Thereafter, a state court suit was begun pursuant to a comprehensive state water adjudication scheme.

Issue: Did the federal court have jurisdiction? Should it have abstained?

Held: (1) The federal courts have jurisdiction under 28 U.S.C. § 1345, the general provision covering civil actions brought by the federal government.

(2) Under the McCarran Amendment, whereby the United States waived its sovereign immunity in water rights adjudications, the state court has concurrent jurisdiction.

(3) Although the doctrine of abstention does not apply, the federal court should nevertheless defer to state adjudication in the interests of "wise judicial administration." The factors supporting federal court deference are the infancy of the federal proceedings, the "extensive involvement" of state water rights, the distance from the federal court to the region under consideration, the willingness of the federal government to participate in other, similar proceedings, and the McCarran Amendment's policy to avoid "piecemeal adjudication of water rights."

(4) No "substantive claim on behalf of Indians under the doctrine of reserved rights" is abridged. The state forum must still apply federal law, and these federal questions are reviewable by the Supreme Court.

6. *Colville Confederated Tribes v. Walton,* 647 F.2d 42 (9th Cir.), *cert. denied,* 454 U.S. 1092 (1981).

Facts: A non-Indian purchased three allotments from an Indian, who had previously begun to irrigate the land. The non-Indian continued to divert water from the nearby creek located solely on the reservation.

Issues: Can an Indian allottee transfer Indian water rights to a non-Indian? Is change of use permissible for *Winters* rights? Can Indian water rights be used to maintain a tribal fishery stocked with non-indigenous fish?

Held: (1) The "purpose" for which the reservation was established--"a home for the Indians"--is liberally construed to benefit the Tribe. The Tribe has a reserved right to enough water to maintain its fishery.

(2) "Change of use is permissible." The Tribe has "a vested right in reserved water [which] it may use in any lawful manner."

(3) "Indian allottees have a right to use reserved water," and "an Indian allottee may sell his right to reserved water."

(4) "The extent of an Indian allottee's right is based on the number of irrigable acres he owns" (i.e., the "ratable share"). The priority date is "the date the reservation was created." In the event there is insufficient water to satisfy all valid claims to reserved water, the amount of reserved water to each claimant is reduced proportionately. These principles are passed on to the non-Indian purchaser.

(5) But whereas "the Indian allottee does not lose by non-use the right to a share of reserved water," the non-Indian purchaser acquires only the right to "water being appropriated by the Indian allottee at the time title passes . . . and water he or she appropriates with reasonable diligence after the passage of title." These rights can be lost by non-use.

(6) "The state has no power to regulate" water rights located solely on the reservation. State control was preempted when the reservation was established.

7. *Nevada v. United States*, 463 U.S. 110 (1983).

Facts: The "Orr Ditch Litigation" adjudicated water rights to the Truckee River for the benefit of both the Tribe and a "reclamation project." The federal government represented both against all other uses of the river's water. Subsequently, the federal government and the Tribe brought another action for water rights to support a fishery on the reservation, claiming that the first action only resolved water rights for irrigation purposes. The defendants in the second action were the original defendants or their successors and the new managers of the reclamation project.

Issue: Was the second suit barred by res judicata?

Held: (1) Congress obliged the Secretary of the Interior both to fulfill the "fiduciary obligation" to the Tribe and the statutory obligations to the reclamation project. In such circumstances, the Secretary's "trust obligations" cannot be adjudged by "the fastidious standards of a private fiduciary." Thus, the government's representation of potentially conflicting interests was permissible.

(2) Res judicata binds the "parties and those in privity with them" when a final judgment is entered on the merits of a case. The reservation's "active water right to the Truckee" was litigated in *Orr Ditch,* and neither the United States nor the Tribe ("whose interests were represented") can relitigate that cause of action.

(3) The interests of the Tribe and the reclamation project were "sufficiently adverse" in the *Orr Ditch* litigation so that both are bound by that decision even though they were represented by the same party.

(4) Even defendants who appropriated Truckee water after *Orr Ditch* can rely on res judicata, despite the absence of "mutuality." Because "everyone involved in *Orr Ditch* contemplated a comprehensive adjudication of water rights," even non-parties need to rely on that decree.

8. *Arizona v. San Carlos Apache Tribe,* 463 U.S. 545 (1983).

Facts: The federal government and Indian tribes filed suits in federal court to adjudicate water rights in certain streams and rivers. Non-Indian water claimants filed suit in state court. The state enabling acts disclaimed all jurisdiction over Indian lands. The McCarran Act did not mention Indian tribes.

Issue: Did the McCarran Act require federal courts to defer to state courts in suits brought by tribes, as well as in those brought by the federal government? Did the enabling act's disclaimer prevent state court jurisdiction?

Held: (1) The federal courts had jurisdiction to hear suits brought by the United States and by the tribes, under 28 U.S.C §§ 1345 and 1362.

(2) The disclaimers of state jurisdiction in the enabling acts "were removed by the McCarran Amendment" insofar as state adjudication over water rights is concerned.

(3) The rule in *Colorado River* of federal court deference to state courts in water rights adjudications applies to cases brought by tribes. "Duplicative and wasteful" litigation is to be avoided. But "any state court decision alleged to abridge Indian water rights protected by federal law" will receive "particularized and exacting scrutiny" by the Supreme Court.

(4) Federal courts need not defer to the state proceedings if (i) the state courts defer, (ii) the federal suit is "well enough along," or (iii) in a "closely matched" situation, Indian rights tip the balance in favor of federal adjudication rather than state.

9. *Arizona v. California (II),* 460 U.S. 605 (1983).

Facts: The United States and the five tribes sought increased water rights for the reservations on the grounds that certain irrigable lands were not accounted for in the earlier litigation and reservation boundary lines had been finally resolved with increased irrigable acreage.

Issue: Could the tribes intervene? Were the omitted lands barred from consideration by the previous court decree? Had the boundaries of the reservations been finally determined so that additional water rights could be allocated to the tribes?

Held: (1) The tribes' intervention does not violate the states' immunity under the Eleventh Amendment. No claims are raised which differ from those raised by the United States.

(2) Although res judicata does not apply, because this is an original action before the Supreme Court in which the Court has maintained jurisdiction to modify its decree, the "strong interest in finality" prevents the omitted lands issue from being raised. The calculation of the amount of "practically irrigable acreage" will thus not be reopened.

(3) There was no conflict of interest just because the United States represented other federal property interests as well as the tribes in the earlier action, and even though the government erred in calculating the irrigable acreage. There was "no indication that the government's representation . . . was legally inadequate."

(4) The reservation boundaries established by Secretarial Order are not "final determinations." Thus, the enlarged tribal water rights will not be recognized until judicial adjudication of the boundary issue is complete. Where judicial determinations have been made, those boundary determinations are final and the tribes' water rights can be increased.

10. *United States v. Adair,* 723 F.2d 1394 (9th Cir.), *cert. denied,* 467 U.S. 1252 (1984).

Facts: The United States filed suit to determine the water rights in the area of the former Klamath Indian Reservation. The Reservation was disposed of in accordance with the Klamath Termination Act. Most of the land was acquired by the United States Forest Service. The Klamath Tribe retained the right to hunt and fish in the former reservation area.

Issue: What were the water rights of the Klamath Tribe and their priority?

Held: (1) "The [district] court limited its determination to ordering the priority among reserved water rights arising under federal law," and thus correctly exercised jurisdiction.

(2) Implied water rights arise when they are needed to fulfill the purposes of a federal reservation. "[A]t the time the Klamath Reservation was established, the Government and the Tribe intended to reserve a quantity of water flowing through the reservation not only for the purpose of supporting Klamath agriculture, but also

for the purpose of maintaining the Tribe's treaty right to hunt and fish on reservation lands." These rights survived termination.

(3) "[W]ithin the 1864 Treaty is a recognition of the Tribe's aboriginal water rights . . . [which] necessarily carry a priority date of time immemorial."

(4) The Tribe is entitled to "the amount of water necessary to support its hunting and fishing rights as currently exercised to maintain the livelihood of Tribal members, not as these rights once were exercised by the Tribe in 1864."

11. *United States v. Anderson,* 736 F.2d 1358 (9th Cir. 1984).

Facts: The United States filed suit to initiate a general adjudication of water rights in the Chamokane Basin. Waters of the Basin are not wholly within the Spokane Indian Reservation. The Spokane Indian Reservation includes Indian tribal and allotment lands which have never left trust status, land owned in fee by non-Indians, and lands which left trust status and were later reacquired by the Tribe and returned to trust status.

Issue: What are the priority dates of water rights appurtenant to lands within the Spokane Indian Reservation? What governmental entity has jurisdiction to regulate the allocation of excess water rights within the reservation and appurtenant to non-Indian lands?

Held: (1) "[T]he establishment of the [Indian] reservation implies a right to sufficient unappropriated water to accomplish its purpose. . . . These tribal reserved *Winters* rights vest on the date of the creation of the Indian reservation."

(2) "[A] non-Indian successor [to an Indian allottee] acquires a right to that quantity of water being utilized at the time title passes, plus that amount of water which the successor puts to beneficial use with reasonable diligence following the transfer of title." If all of the water right is not acquired and maintained through continued use by the successor, then "the Tribe reacquires only those rights which have not been lost through nonuse and those rights will have an original, date-of-the-reservation priority."

(3) Homesteaders acquire no federal water rights and must rely on the appropriation doctrine to acquire water rights. If the homesteader has no perfected water rights, there are no rights to be acquired by the Tribe when the Tribe reacquires the land formerly opened to homesteading. But upon reacquisition and return to trust status, "we hold that the Tribe is entitled to an implication of *Winters* rights with a priority for these rights as of the date of reacquisition, rather than an original, date-of-the-reservation priority."

(4) Tribal sovereignty limits state regulatory jurisdiction over non-Indian activities on an Indian reservation. However, the state may regulate non-Indian activities on non-Indian fee lands within the reservation, unless those activities arise from conducting business with the tribe or its members, or they threaten the political integrity, economic security, or health or welfare of the tribe. After considering the interests involved, "it is clear that the state may exercise its regulatory jurisdiction over the use of surplus, non-reserved Chamokane Basin waters by nonmembers on non-Indian fee lands within the Spokane Indian Reservation." Tribal interests will not be infringed because the Tribe's reserved rights "have been quantified and will be protected by the federal water master."

12. *In re the General Adjudication of All Rights To Use Water In the Big Horn River System and All Other Sources, State of Wyoming*, 753 P.2d 76 (Wyo. 1988), *aff'd by an equally divided court*, 492 U.S. ___, 106 L. Ed. 2d 342 (1989).

Facts: The State of Wyoming filed suit to initiate a general adjudication of all rights to use water in the Big Horn River System and all other sources. The parties included the United States and the Shoshone and Arapahoe Tribes of the Wind River Indian Reservation.

Issue: What water rights were reserved to the Wind River Indian Reservation when it was created by the United States?

Held: (1) The Wyoming State Constitution contains a disclaimer of title and jurisdiction over Indian lands within state boundaries. However, the disclaimer must be interpreted consistent with federal law. Because the McCarran Amendment allows state courts to adjudicate Indian water rights as part of general stream adjudications, the constitutional disclaimer does not prevent Wyoming from adjudicating Indian water rights on the Big Horn River System.

(2) The amount of water impliedly reserved for an Indian reservation "is determined by the purposes for which the reservation was created." As a matter of law, the purpose of the reservation can be determined from the language of the treaty creating the reservation. "Although the treaty did not force the Indians to become farmers and although it clearly contemplates that other activities would be permitted (hunting is mentioned in Article 4, lumbering and milling in Article 3, roaming in Article 9), the treaty encouraged only agriculture, and that was its primary purpose." In addition, the trial court found no dependency upon fishing nor a traditional fishing lifestyle. "The evidence is not sufficient to imply a fishery flow right absent a treaty provision."

(3) "[W]e hold that the reserved water doctrine does not extend to groundwater. . . ."

(4) The appropriate measure for quantifying the Tribes' reserved water right is that amount of water necessary to irrigate all of the reservation's practically irrigable acreage.

(5) Reservation lands, lands currently held by Indian allottees, and lands which had passed out of Indian ownership but have been reacquired by a tribal or individual tribal member purchaser, all are entitled to a priority dating from the establishment of the reservation--1868.

(6) Non-Indian successors to Indian allottees "must be awarded a reserved water right with an 1868 priority date for the PIA [practically irrigable acreage] they can show were irrigated by their Indian predecessors or put under irrigation within a reasonable time thereafter."

(7) "[E]xercise of the [Indian] reserved water rights are [sic] intimately bound up with the state water rights of off-reservation users." Because federal law has not preempted state oversight of reserved water rights, the state engineer has the authority to enforce the decree against state appropriators.

TABLE OF CASES

TOPICAL TABLE OF CASES

II.A. The Federal-Indian Governmental Relationship

II.B. The Federal-Indian Statutory Relationship

II.C. The Federal-Indian Individual Relationship

II.D. The Federal-Indian Trust Relationship

III.A.1. General Civil Jurisdiction

III.A.2. Regulatory Civil Jurisdiction

III.A.3. Domestic Civil Jurisdiction

III.B. Criminal Jurisdiction

III.C. Tax Jurisdiction

IV.A. Indian Reserved Rights: Indian Treaties

IV.B. Indian Reserved Rights: Indian Lands

IV.C. Indian Reserved Hunting and Fishing Rights

IV.D. Indian Reserved Water Rights

INDEX